Basic Computation Series 2000

Working with Percents

Loretta M. Taylor, Ed. D.

Harold D. Taylor, Ed. D.

Dale Seymour Publications®
Parsippany, New Jersey

Executive Editor: Catherine Anderson

Editorial Manager: John Nelson

Development Editor: Deborah J. Slade

**Production/Manufacturing
Director:** Janet Yearian

**Sr. Production/Manufacturing
Coordinator:** Roxanne Knoll

Design Director: Jim O'Shea

Design Manager: Jeff Kelly

Cover Designer: Monika Popowitz

Interior Designer: Christy Butterfield

Composition: Claire Flaherty

This book is published by Dale Seymour Publications®, an imprint of Pearson Learning.

Dale Seymour Publications
299 Jefferson Road
Parsippany, NJ 07054-0480
Customer Service: 800-872-1100

ISBN 0-7690-0118-1
Order Number DS21920

2 3 4 5 6 7 8 9 10–ML–03 02 01

This Book Is Printed
On Recycled Paper

Authors of the Basic Computation Series 2000

Loretta M. Taylor is a retired high school mathematics teacher. During her teaching career, she taught at Hillsdale High School in San Mateo, California; Crestmoor High School in San Bruno, California; Patterson High School in Patterson, California; Round Valley Union High School in Covelo, California; and Farmington High School in Farmington, New Mexico. Dr. Taylor obtained a B.S. in mathematics from Southeastern Oklahoma State University, and both an M.A. in mathematics and an Ed.D. in mathematics education from the University of Northern Colorado. She has been active in professional organizations at the local, state, and national levels, including the National Council of Teachers of Mathematics, the California Mathematics Council, the National Education Association, and the California Teachers Association. She has given a variety of talks and workshops at numerous conferences, schools, and universities. Dr. Taylor is a member of Lambda Sigma Tau, a national honorary science fraternity, and is coauthor of *Paper and Scissors Polygons and More, Algebra Book 1, Algebra Book 2,* and *Developing Skills in Algebra 1.* In retirement, she continues to be an active mathematics author and is involved with community organizations.

Harold D. Taylor is a retired high school mathematics teacher, having taught at Aragon High School in San Mateo, California; as well as at Patterson High School in Patterson, California; Round Valley Union High School in Covelo, California; and Farmington High School in Farmington, New Mexico. He has served in high schools not only as a mathematics teacher, but also as a mathematics department head and as an assistant principal. He received a B.S. in mathematics from Southeastern Oklahoma State University, and both an M.A. in mathematics and an Ed.D. in mathematics education from the University of Northern Colorado. Dr. Taylor has been very active in a number of professional organizations, having worked in a variety of significant capacities for the National Council of Teachers of Mathematics and the California Mathematics Council. He was chairman of the Publicity and Information Committee and the Local Organizing Committee for the Fourth International Congress on Mathematics Education at Berkeley, California, was on the writing team of the California Assessment Test, and was a member of the California State Mathematics Framework and Criteria Committee, chairing the California State Mathematics Framework Addendum Committee. Since 1966, he has spoken at more than one hundred local, state, and national meetings on mathematics and mathematics education. Dr. Taylor is author of *Ten Mathematics Projects and Career Education Infusion,* and coauthor of *Algebra Book 1, Algebra Book 2,* and *Developing Skills in Algebra 1.* In 1989 he was the California recipient of the Presidential Award for Excellence in Teaching Secondary Mathematics. In retirement, Dr. Taylor is continuing to produce mathematics materials for the classroom, and also serves his community as County Judge in Custer County, Colorado, having been appointed to this position by Governor Roy Romer.

Table of Contents

A Note of Introduction

To the Teacher

Some students are familiar with computational work but have never really mastered it. Perhaps this is a result of a lack of practice. With the *Basic Computation Series 2000,* you can provide students with as much practice as they need. You can teach, check up, reteach, and reinforce. You can give classwork and homework. If you wish, you can create a full year's course in basic computation, or you can provide skills maintenance when it's needed. All the work is here. Select the pages you want to use for the students who need them.

To the Student

You can't play a guitar before you learn the chords. You can't shoot a hook shot before you learn the lay-up. You can't pass a mathematics exam before you learn to compute, and you can't master computational skills until you learn the mathematical facts and procedures. Learning takes practice; there are no shortcuts. The pages in this book are for practice. Do your math every day and think about what you're doing. If you don't understand something, ask questions. Don't do too much work in your head; it's worth an extra sheet of paper to write down your steps. Also, be patient with yourself. Learning takes time.

Although calculators and other computational devices are readily available to most everyone, you will be forever handicapped if you are not able to perform basic mathematical computations without the aid of a mechanical or electronic computational device. Learn and master the procedures so that you can rely on your own abilities.

To the Parent

The importance of the development of mathematical skills cannot be emphasized enough. Mathematics is needed to estimate materials for a construction job or to price a car. It's needed to predict earthquakes and to prescribe medicine. It helps you determine how to stretch your dollars and pay your bills. This program provides the practice students need to develop the essential computational skills. Conventional algorithms are utilized throughout the *Basic Computation Series 2000.* You can help your children learn these skills. Give them your support and encouragement. Urge them to do their homework. Be there to answer their questions. Give them a quiet place to work. Make them feel good about trying. Your help can make the difference.

About the Program

What is the Basic Computation Series 2000?

The books in the *Basic Computation Series 2000* provide comprehensive practice on all the essential computational skills. There are nine practice books and a test book. The practice books consist of carefully sequenced drill worksheets organized in groups of five. The test book contains daily quizzes (160 quizzes in all), semester tests, and year-end tests written in standardized-test format.

Book 1	Working with Whole Numbers
Book 2	Understanding Fractions
Book 3	Working with Fractions
Book 4	Working with Decimals
Book 5	Working with Percents
Book 6	Understanding Measurement
Book 7	Working with Perimeter and Area
Book 8	Working with Surface Area and Volume
Book 9	Applying Computational Skills
Test Book 10	Basic Computation Quizzes and Tests

Who can use the Basic Computation Series 2000?

The *Basic Computation Series 2000* is appropriate for use by any person, young or old, who has not achieved computational proficiency. It may be used with any program calling for carefully sequenced computational practice. The material is especially suitable for use with students in fifth grade, middle school, junior high school, special education classes, and high school. It may be used by classroom teachers, substitute teachers, tutors, and parents. It is also useful for those in adult education, for those preparing for the General Education Development Test (GED), and for others wishing to study on their own.

What is in this book?

This book is a practice book. In addition to explanation and examples for the student, parent, and teacher, it contains student worksheets, answers, and a record sheet.

Worksheets

The worksheets are designed to give even the slowest student a chance to master the essential computational skills. Most worksheets come in five equivalent forms allowing for pretesting, practice, and post-testing on any particular skill. Each set of worksheets provides practice on only one or two specific skills, and the work progresses in very small steps from one set to the next. Instructions are clear and simple. Ample practice is provided on each page, giving students the opportunity to strengthen their skills. Answers to each problem are included in the back of the book.

Explanatory Material

The beginning of each section includes explanatory material designed to help students, parents, and teachers understand the material in the section and its purpose. Fully-worked examples show how to work each type of exercise. The example solutions are written in a straightforward manner so as to be easily understood.

Student Record Sheet

A record sheet is provided to help in recording progress and assessing instructional needs.

Answers

Answers to all problems are included in the back of the book.

How can the Basic Computation Series 2000 be used?

The materials in the *Basic Computation Series 2000* can serve as the major skeleton of a skills program or as supplements to any other computational skills program. The large number of worksheets provides a wide variety from which to choose and allows flexibility in structuring a program to meet individual needs. The following suggestions are offered to show how the *Basic Computation Series 2000* may be adapted to a particular situation.

Minimal Competency Practice

In various fields and schools, standardized tests are used for entrance, passage from one level to another, and certification of competency or proficiency prior to graduation. The materials in the *Basic Computation Series 2000* are particularly well-suited to preparing for any of the various mathematics competency tests, including the mathematics portion of the General Education Development Test (GED) used to certify high school equivalency.

Together, the books in the *Basic Computation Series 2000* provide practice in all the essential computational skills measured on competency tests. The semester tests and year-end tests from the test book are written in standardized-test format. These tests can be used as sample minimal competency tests. The worksheets can be used to brush up on skills measured by the competency tests.

Skills Maintenance

Since most worksheets come in five equivalent forms, the work can be organized into weekly units as suggested by the following schedule: A five-day schedule can begin on any day of the week. The authors' ideal schedule begins on Thursday, with pretesting and introduction of a skill, and follows with reteaching on Friday. Monday and Tuesday are for practice, touch-up teaching, reinforcing, and individualized instruction. Wednesday is test day. Daily quizzes from the *Basic Computation Series 2000 Quizzes And Tests Book* can be used on the drill-and-practice days for maintenance of previously-learned skills or diagnosis of skill deficiencies. Ideally, except for test days, a quiz may be given during the first fifteen minutes of a class period with the remainder of the period used for instruction and practice with other materials.

Authors' Suggested Teaching Schedule

	Day 1	Day 2	Day 3	Day 4	Day 5
Week 1	Pages 5 and 6	Pages 7 and 8	Pages 9 and 10	Pages 11 and 12	Pages 13 and 14
	Pages 15 and 16	Pages 17 and 18	Pages 19 and 20	Pages 21 and 22	Pages 23 and 24
Week 2	Pages 25 and 26	Pages 27 and 28	Pages 29 and 30	Pages 31 and 32	Pages 33 and 34
	Pages 35 and 36	Pages 37 and 38	Pages 39 and 40	Pages 41 and 42	Pages 43 and 44
Week 3	Pages 47 and 48	Pages 49 and 50	Pages 51 and 52	Pages 53 and 54	Pages 55 and 56
	Pages 57 and 58	Pages 59 and 60	Pages 61 and 62	Pages 63 and 64	Pages 65 and 66
Week 4	Pages 71 and 72	Pages 73 and 74	Pages 75 and 76	Pages 77 and 78	Pages 79 and 80
	Pages 81 and 82	Pages 83 and 84	Pages 85 and 86	Pages 87 and 88	Pages 89 and 90

Supplementary Drill

There are more than 18,000 problems in the *Basic Computation Series 2000*. When students need more practice with a given skill, use the appropriate worksheets from the series. They are suitable for classwork or homework practice following the teaching of a specific skill. With five equivalent pages for most worksheets, adequate practice is provided for each essential skill.

How are the materials prepared?

The books are designed with pages that can be easily reproduced. Permanent transparencies can be produced using a copy machine and special transparencies designed for this purpose. The program will run more smoothly if the student's work is stored in folders. Record sheets can be attached to the folders so that students, teachers, or parents can keep records of an individual's progress. Materials stored in this way are readily available for conferences with the student or parent.

Student Record Sheet

Worksheets Completed

Page Number

5	7	9	11		13
6	8	10	12		14
15	17	19	21		23
16	18	20	22		24
25	27	29	31		33
26	28	30	32		34
35	37	39	41		43
36	38	40	42		44
47	49	51	53		55
48	50	52	54		56
57	59	61	63		65
58	60	62	64		66
71	73	75	77		79
72	74	76	78		80
81	83	85	87		89
82	84	86	88		90

Quiz Grades

No.	Score

Checklist

Skill Mastered	Date
❏ converting percents to fractions and decimals	
❏ converting fractions to decimals and percents	
❏ fractional part of a number	
❏ common fraction-to-percent equivalencies	
❏ finding percentages	
❏ working with sales tax	
❏ finding rates	
❏ finding bases	
❏ finding rates, bases, and percentages	
❏ discounts	
❏ sales	
❏ hotel statements	

Notes

_____

_____

_____

_____

_____

_____

Decimals, Fractions, and Percents

There are three kinds of fractions that are commonly used, common fractions, decimal fractions, and percents. Book 3 deals primarily with common fractions, Book 4 with decimal fractions, and Book 5, this book, deals primarily with percents, stressing the relationship among these three types of fractions.

Percent means *hundredths.* In fact, 14% is the same as 0.14 or $\frac{14}{100}$. The percent symbol, "%," suggests a fraction bar and a denominator of 100. To write a percent as a common fraction, drop the percent sign and replace it with 100 in the denominator of a common fraction. To write a percent as a decimal, drop the percent sign and divide the number by 100; that is, move the decimal point two places to the left.

Example 1: Write 57% as a fraction with a denominator of 100.

Solution: Replace the % sign with a fraction bar and write a denominator of 100. Thus, $57\% = \frac{57}{100}$.

Example 2: Write 45% as a fraction in simplest form.

Solution: $45\% = \frac{45}{100}$

$$\frac{45}{100} = \frac{3 \times 3 \times 5}{2 \times 2 \times 5 \times 5}$$

Divide common factors from the numerator and denominator, and multiply the remaining factors to get the reduced fraction.

$$\frac{3 \times 3 \times \cancel{5}}{2 \times 2 \times 5 \times \cancel{5}} = \frac{9}{20}$$

Thus, $45\% = \frac{9}{20}$.

Example 3: **a.** Write 225% in decimal form.

b. Write $37\frac{1}{2}\%$ in decimal form.

Solution: **a.** Drop the percent sign and move the decimal point two places to the left. Thus, 225% = 2.25.

b. Drop the percent sign and move the decimal point two places to the left. Thus, $37\frac{1}{2}\%$ (which is the same as 37.5%) is equal to $0.37\frac{1}{2}$, or 0.375. However, it is not good form to use both a common fraction and a decimal in the representation of a number, so 0.375 is preferable.

Example 4: Write $\frac{84}{100}$ as a fraction in simplest form.

Solution: Write the numerator and denominator in prime factored form.

$$\frac{84}{100} = \frac{2 \times 2 \times 3 \times 7}{2 \times 2 \times 5 \times 5}$$

Divide common factors from the numerator and denominator, and multiply the remaining factors to get the reduced fraction.

$$\frac{\cancel{2} \times \cancel{2} \times 3 \times 7}{\cancel{2} \times \cancel{2} \times 5 \times 5} = \frac{21}{25}$$

Thus, in simplest form, $\frac{84}{100} = \frac{21}{25}$.

Example 5: Write $\frac{35}{100}$ in decimal form.

Solution: To divide 35 by 100, move the decimal point two places to the left. Thus, $\frac{35}{100} = 0.35$.

To write a common fraction or a decimal fraction as a percent, multiply the fraction by 100 and annex a percent sign.

Example 6: **a.** Write $\frac{13}{100}$ in percent form.

   b. Write $\frac{185}{100}$ in percent form.

Solution: **a.** To write $\frac{13}{100}$ in percent form, multiply $\frac{13}{100}$ by 100 and annex a percent sign. Thus, $\frac{13}{100} = 13\%$.

   b. To write $\frac{185}{100}$ in percent form, multiply $\frac{185}{100}$ by 100 and annex a percent sign. Thus, $\frac{185}{100} = 185\%$.

Example 7: Find $\frac{7}{5}$ of 85. Write the answer in simplest form.

Solution: Since $\frac{7}{5}$ "of" 85 means $\frac{7}{5} \times 85$, write the problem so that 85 is the numerator of a fraction whose denominator is 1 and reduce the product.

$$\frac{7}{5} \times \frac{85}{1} = \frac{7}{\cancel{5}} \times \frac{\cancel{5} \times 17}{1} = 119$$

Thus, $\frac{7}{5}$ of 85 is 119.

Example 8: Find 163% of 74.

Solution: In percent problems, "of" means multiplication, the same as it does in fraction or decimal problems. However, a number written as a percent cannot be used in computation; it must be converted to fraction or decimal form. Write 163% as 1.63 and then multiply.

$$1.63 \times 74 = 120.62$$

Thus, 163% of 74 is 120.62.

Example 9: Write $\frac{3}{8}$ as a percent.

Solution: Multiply $\frac{3}{8}$ by 100.

$$\frac{3}{8} \times \frac{100}{1} = \frac{3}{2 \times 2 \times 2} \times \frac{2 \times 2 \times 5 \times 5}{1} = \frac{75}{2}$$

Method 1: $\frac{75}{2} = 37\frac{1}{2}$; thus, $\frac{3}{8} = 37\frac{1}{2}\%$.

Method 2: $\frac{75}{2} = 37.5$; thus, $\frac{3}{8} = 37.5\%$.

Example 10: Write $\frac{1}{3}$ as a percent.

Solution: Multiply $\frac{1}{3}$ by 100.

$$\frac{1}{3} \times \frac{100}{1} = \frac{100}{3} = 33\frac{1}{3}$$

Thus, $\frac{1}{3} = 33\frac{1}{3}\%$.

Since it is true that $\frac{1}{3} \times 100 = 33.\overline{3}$, this answer could also be written $33.\overline{3}\%$.

The two methods used in Examples 9 and 10 produce equivalent percents and can be used interchangeably. An answer given in one form is just as valid as the answer written in the other form. In completing some computations, one form may be preferable to the other.

Example 11: Find 75% of 32.

Solution: Write 75% as a common fraction or as a decimal fraction and multiply.

Method 1: Write 75% as 0.75 and multiply.

Thus, 75% of 32 = 0.75 × 32, which is 24.

Method 2: Write $\frac{75}{100}$ as $\frac{3}{4}$ and multiply.

Since $\frac{3}{4} \times 32 = 24$, 75% of 32 is 24.

When completing a problem like Example 11 where the percent is equivalent to a common fraction that is easy to use in computation, it may be preferable to use Method 2. Be sure to assess the problem and use the method that will make the computation easiest.

Example 12: Find $33\frac{1}{3}\%$ of 42.

Solution: The computation will be easier if the fraction $\frac{1}{3}$ is used for $33\frac{1}{3}\%$. Therefore, multiply 42 by $\frac{1}{3}$.

$$\frac{1}{3} \times \frac{42}{1} = \frac{1}{3} \times \frac{2 \times 3 \times 7}{1} = 14$$

Thus, $33\frac{1}{3}\%$ of 42 is 14.

One common application for percents involves *sales tax*. Sales tax is collected in most areas of the United States. In some areas sales tax is not charged on food or clothes; in other areas it is. The rate at which sales tax is charged is almost always expressed as a percent. The amount of sales tax is calculated by finding the specified percent of the purchase price. The total amount charged the customer is the amount of the purchase plus the amount of sales tax.

Example 13: The sales tax charged in a certain county is 6.5%. For each of the following purchases, find the amount of sales tax charged on the purchase and the total cost of the purchase. Round each answer to the nearest cent.

    a. $37.50

    b. $56.10

Solution: **a.** To find 6.5% of $37.50, change 6.5% to 0.065, and multiply.

$$37.50 \times 0.065 = 2.4375$$

Rounding to the nearest cent, the sales tax is $2.44. Since $37.50 + $2.44 = $39.94, the total cost of the purchase is $39.94.

    b. To find 6.5% of $56.10, change 6.5% to 0.065, and multiply.

$$56.10 \times 0.065 = 3.6465$$

Rounding to the nearest cent, the sales tax is $3.65. Since $56.10 + $3.65 = $59.75, the total cost of the purchase is $59.75.

Converting Percents to Fractions and Decimals

Complete the chart.

	percent form	fraction (denominator of 100)	fraction (lowest terms)	decimal form
1.	24%	$\frac{24}{100}$	$\frac{6}{25}$	0.24
2.	56%			
3.	92%			
4.	105%			
5.	69%			
6.	53%			
7.	28%			
8.	75%			
9.	25%			
10.	50%			
11.	$33\frac{1}{3}$%			
12.	32%			
13.	145%			
14.	$62\frac{1}{2}$%			
15.	176%			
16.	225%			
17.	95%			
18.	42%			
19.	265%			
20.	67%			

Converting Fractions to Decimals and Percents

Complete the chart.

	fraction (denominator of 100)	fraction (lowest terms)	decimal form	percent form
1.	$\frac{50}{100}$	$\frac{1}{2}$	0.50	50%
2.	$\frac{25}{100}$			
3.	$\frac{175}{100}$			
4.	$\frac{140}{100}$			
5.	$\frac{240}{100}$			
6.	$\frac{170}{100}$			
7.	$\frac{55}{100}$			
8.	$\frac{135}{100}$			
9.	$\frac{185}{100}$			
10.	$\frac{204}{100}$			
11.	$\frac{125}{100}$			
12.	$\frac{12}{100}$			
13.	$\frac{56}{100}$			
14.	$\frac{88}{100}$			
15.	$\frac{96}{100}$			
16.	$\frac{144}{100}$			
17.	$\frac{176}{100}$			
18.	$\frac{212}{100}$			
19.	$\frac{20}{100}$			
20.	$\frac{45}{100}$			

Converting Percents to Fractions and Decimals

Complete the chart.

percent form	fraction (denominator of 100)	fraction (lowest terms)	decimal form
1. 68%	$\frac{68}{100}$	$\frac{17}{25}$	0.68
2. 73%			
3. 46%			
4. 29%			
5. 50%			
6. 34%			
7. 26%			
8. 81%			
9. 49%			
10. 56%			
11. 59%			
12. 98%			
13. 156%			
14. 216%			
15. 44%			
16. 114%			
17. 29%			
18. 32%			
19. 67%			
20. $37\frac{1}{2}$%			

Converting Fractions to Decimals and Percents

Complete the chart.

	fraction (denominator of 100)	fraction (lowest terms)	decimal form	percent form
1.	$\frac{245}{100}$	$\frac{49}{20}$	2.45	245%
2.	$\frac{85}{100}$			
3.	$\frac{180}{100}$			
4.	$\frac{16}{100}$			
5.	$\frac{120}{100}$			
6.	$\frac{270}{100}$			
7.	$\frac{304}{100}$			
8.	$\frac{155}{100}$			
9.	$\frac{35}{100}$			
10.	$\frac{70}{100}$			
11.	$\frac{225}{100}$			
12.	$\frac{150}{100}$			
13.	$\frac{132}{100}$			
14.	$\frac{176}{100}$			
15.	$\frac{32}{100}$			
16.	$\frac{52}{100}$			
17.	$\frac{128}{100}$			
18.	$\frac{20}{100}$			
19.	$\frac{30}{100}$			
20.	$\frac{230}{100}$			

Converting Percents to Fractions and Decimals

Complete the chart.

percent form	fraction (denominator of 100)	fraction (lowest terms)	decimal form
1. 35%	$\frac{35}{100}$	$\frac{7}{20}$	0.35
2. 60%			
3. 42%			
4. 28%			
5. 39%			
6. $37\frac{1}{2}$%			
7. 40%			
8. 76%			
9. 53%			
10. 75%			
11. 65%			
12. $33\frac{1}{3}$%			
13. 72%			
14. 150%			
15. 47%			
16. 12%			
17. 175%			
18. 67%			
19. $12\frac{1}{2}$%			
20. 85%			

Converting Fractions to Decimals and Percents

Complete the chart.

	fraction (denominator of 100)	fraction (lowest terms)	decimal form	percent form
1.	$\frac{80}{100}$	$\frac{4}{5}$	0.80	80%
2.	$\frac{95}{100}$			
3.	$\frac{255}{100}$			
4.	$\frac{110}{100}$			
5.	$\frac{105}{100}$			
6.	$\frac{215}{100}$			
7.	$\frac{168}{100}$			
8.	$\frac{112}{100}$			
9.	$\frac{44}{100}$			
10.	$\frac{136}{100}$			
11.	$\frac{275}{100}$			
12.	$\frac{25}{100}$			
13.	$\frac{5}{100}$			
14.	$\frac{84}{100}$			
15.	$\frac{188}{100}$			
16.	$\frac{225}{100}$			
17.	$\frac{250}{100}$			
18.	$\frac{160}{100}$			
19.	$\frac{65}{100}$			
20.	$\frac{220}{100}$			

Converting Percents to Fractions and Decimals

Complete the chart.

percent form	fraction (denominator of 100)	fraction (lowest terms)	decimal form
1. 102%	$\frac{102}{100}$	$\frac{51}{50}$	1.02
2. 53%			
3. 30%			
4. 36%			
5. 69%			
6. 20%			
7. 5%			
8. 38%			
9. 25%			
10. 84%			
11. 62%			
12. 115%			
13. 48%			
14. 34%			
15. 81%			
16. $66\frac{2}{3}$%			
17. 325%			
18. $37\frac{1}{2}$%			
19. 155%			
20. $12\frac{1}{2}$%			

Converting Fractions to Decimals and Percents

Complete the chart.

	fraction (denominator of 100)	fraction (lowest terms)	decimal form	percent form
1.	$\frac{20}{100}$	$\frac{1}{5}$	0.20	20%
2.	$\frac{140}{100}$			
3.	$\frac{150}{100}$			
4.	$\frac{210}{100}$			
5.	$\frac{145}{100}$			
6.	$\frac{115}{100}$			
7.	$\frac{76}{100}$			
8.	$\frac{176}{100}$			
9.	$\frac{8}{100}$			
10.	$\frac{75}{100}$			
11.	$\frac{175}{100}$			
12.	$\frac{90}{100}$			
13.	$\frac{180}{100}$			
14.	$\frac{205}{100}$			
15.	$\frac{148}{100}$			
16.	$\frac{196}{100}$			
17.	$\frac{22}{100}$			
18.	$\frac{24}{100}$			
19.	$\frac{240}{100}$			
20.	$\frac{165}{100}$			

Converting Percents to Fractions and Decimals

Complete the chart.

	percent form	fraction (denominator of 100)	fraction (lowest terms)	decimal form
1.	28%	$\frac{28}{100}$	$\frac{7}{25}$	0.28
2.	41%			
3.	53%			
4.	100%			
5.	48%			
6.	32%			
7.	81%			
8.	40%			
9.	7%			
10.	95%			
11.	82%			
12.	75%			
13.	42%			
14.	250%			
15.	125%			
16.	$33\frac{1}{3}\%$			
17.	145%			
18.	$12\frac{1}{2}\%$			
19.	112%			
20.	43%			

Converting Fractions to Decimals and Percents

Complete the chart.

	fraction (denominator of 100)	fraction (lowest terms)	decimal form	percent form
1.	$\frac{25}{100}$	$\frac{1}{4}$	0.25	25%
2.	$\frac{40}{100}$			
3.	$\frac{10}{100}$			
4.	$\frac{130}{100}$			
5.	$\frac{85}{100}$			
6.	$\frac{125}{100}$			
7.	$\frac{80}{100}$			
8.	$\frac{180}{100}$			
9.	$\frac{185}{100}$			
10.	$\frac{4}{100}$			
11.	$\frac{36}{100}$			
12.	$\frac{104}{100}$			
13.	$\frac{48}{100}$			
14.	$\frac{230}{100}$			
15.	$\frac{124}{100}$			
16.	$\frac{64}{100}$			
17.	$\frac{15}{100}$			
18.	$\frac{275}{100}$			
19.	$\frac{115}{100}$			
20.	$\frac{245}{100}$			

Fractional Part of a Number / Finding Percentages

Complete each of the following.

1. $\frac{1}{2}$ of 42 = _____21_____

2. $\frac{1}{2}$ of 84 = _____

3. $\frac{1}{2}$ of 150 = _____

4. $\frac{1}{2}$ of 28 = _____

5. $\frac{1}{2}$ of 114 = _____

6. $\frac{1}{4}$ of 36 = _____

7. $\frac{1}{4}$ of 48 = _____

8. $\frac{1}{4}$ of 112 = _____

9. $\frac{1}{4}$ of 216 = _____

10. $\frac{1}{4}$ of 200 = _____

11. $\frac{3}{5}$ of 85 = _____

12. $\frac{3}{5}$ of 150 = _____

13. $\frac{3}{5}$ of 55 = _____

14. $\frac{3}{5}$ of 105 = _____

15. $\frac{3}{5}$ of 65 = _____

16. 50% of 42 = _____

17. 50% of 84 = _____

18. 50% of 150 = _____

19. 50% of 28 = _____

20. 50% of 114 = _____

21. 25% of 36 = _____

22. 25% of 48 = _____

23. 25% of 112 = _____

24. 25% of 216 = _____

25. 25% of 200 = _____

26. 60% of 85 = _____

27. 60% of 150 = _____

28. 60% of 55 = _____

29. 60% of 105 = _____

30. 60% of 65 = _____

Fractional Part of a Number / Finding Percentages

Complete each of the following.

1. $\frac{7}{5}$ of 50 = _____70_____

2. $\frac{7}{5}$ of 120 = _____

3. $\frac{7}{5}$ of 115 = _____

4. $\frac{7}{5}$ of 180 = _____

5. $\frac{7}{5}$ of 205 = _____

6. 140% of 50 = _____

7. 140% of 120 = _____

8. 140% of 115 = _____

9. 140% of 180 = _____

10. 140% of 205 = _____

Find each percentage.

11. 36% of 13 = _____4.68_____

12. 51% of 28 = _____

13. 100% of 55 = _____

14. 16% of 56 = _____

15. 120% of 71 = _____

16. 7% of 432 = _____

17. 13% of 27 = _____

18. 27% of 92 = _____

19. 9% of 671 = _____

20. 101% of 65 = _____

Fractional Part of a Number / Finding Percentages

Complete each of the following.

1. $\frac{1}{2}$ of 24 = _____ 12 _____

2. $\frac{1}{2}$ of 92 = _____

3. $\frac{1}{2}$ of 144 = _____

4. $\frac{1}{2}$ of 70 = _____

5. $\frac{1}{2}$ of 68 = _____

6. $\frac{1}{3}$ of 24 = _____

7. $\frac{1}{3}$ of 48 = _____

8. $\frac{1}{3}$ of 144 = _____

9. $\frac{1}{3}$ of 204 = _____

10. $\frac{1}{3}$ of 183 = _____

11. $\frac{4}{5}$ of 15 = _____

12. $\frac{4}{5}$ of 95 = _____

13. $\frac{4}{5}$ of 25 = _____

14. $\frac{4}{5}$ of 150 = _____

15. $\frac{4}{5}$ of 200 = _____

16. 50% of 24 = _____

17. 50% of 92 = _____

18. 50% of 144 = _____

19. 50% of 70 = _____

20. 50% of 68 = _____

21. $33\frac{1}{3}$% of 24 = _____

22. $33\frac{1}{3}$% of 48 = _____

23. $33\frac{1}{3}$% of 144 = _____

24. $33\frac{1}{3}$% of 204 = _____

25. $33\frac{1}{3}$% of 183 = _____

26. 80% of 15 = _____

27. 80% of 95 = _____

28. 80% of 25 = _____

29. 80% of 150 = _____

30. 80% of 200 = _____

Basic Computation Series 2000: Working with Percents
SECTION 1 Decimals, Fractions, and Percents

Fractional Part of a Number / Finding Percentages

Complete each of the following.

1. $\frac{9}{4}$ of 16 = _____36_____

2. $\frac{9}{4}$ of 44 = _____

3. $\frac{9}{4}$ of 116 = _____

4. $\frac{9}{4}$ of 80 = _____

5. $\frac{9}{4}$ of 100 = _____

6. 225% of 16 = _____

7. 225% of 44 = _____

8. 225% of 116 = _____

9. 225% of 80 = _____

10. 225% of 100 = _____

Find each percentage.

11. 52% of 65 = _____33.8_____

12. 142% of 127 = _____

13. 92% of 143 = _____

14. 51% of 89 = _____

15. 27% of 415 = _____

16. 23% of 96 = _____

17. 78% of 32 = _____

18. 81% of 116 = _____

19. 143% of 38 = _____

20. 32% of 345 = _____

Fractional Part of a Number / Finding Percentages

Complete each of the following.

1. $\frac{3}{4}$ of 28 = _____21_____

2. $\frac{3}{4}$ of 80 = _____

3. $\frac{3}{4}$ of 224 = _____

4. $\frac{3}{4}$ of 172 = _____

5. $\frac{3}{4}$ of 364 = _____

6. $\frac{1}{3}$ of 39 = _____

7. $\frac{1}{3}$ of 144 = _____

8. $\frac{1}{3}$ of 99 = _____

9. $\frac{1}{3}$ of 282 = _____

10. $\frac{1}{3}$ of 384 = _____

11. $\frac{3}{8}$ of 72 = _____

12. $\frac{3}{8}$ of 96 = _____

13. $\frac{3}{8}$ of 104 = _____

14. $\frac{3}{8}$ of 32 = _____

15. $\frac{3}{8}$ of 184 = _____

16. 75% of 28 = _____

17. 75% of 80 = _____

18. 75% of 224 = _____

19. 75% of 172 = _____

20. 75% of 364 = _____

21. $33\frac{1}{3}$% of 39 = _____

22. $33\frac{1}{3}$% of 144 = _____

23. $33\frac{1}{3}$% of 99 = _____

24. $33\frac{1}{3}$% of 282 = _____

25. $33\frac{1}{3}$% of 384 = _____

26. $37\frac{1}{2}$% of 72 = _____

27. $37\frac{1}{2}$% of 96 = _____

28. $37\frac{1}{2}$% of 104 = _____

29. $37\frac{1}{2}$% of 32 = _____

30. $37\frac{1}{2}$% of 184 = _____

Fractional Part of a Number / Finding Percentages

Complete each of the following.

1. $\frac{17}{10}$ of 80 = _____136_____

2. $\frac{17}{10}$ of 40 = _____

3. $\frac{17}{10}$ of 200 = _____

4. $\frac{17}{10}$ of 190 = _____

5. $\frac{17}{10}$ of 240 = _____

6. 170% of 80 = _____

7. 170% of 40 = _____

8. 170% of 200 = _____

9. 170% of 190 = _____

10. 170% of 240 = _____

Find each percentage.

11. 37% of 92 = _____34.04_____

12. 93% of 17 = _____

13. 24% of 83 = _____

14. 205% of 55 = _____

15. 98% of 67 = _____

16. 52% of 117 = _____

17. 78% of 62 = _____

18. 143% of 22 = _____

19. 76% of 108 = _____

20. 43% of 39 = _____

Fractional Part of a Number / Finding Percentages

Complete each of the following.

1. $\frac{1}{8}$ of 80 = _____ 10 _____

2. $\frac{1}{8}$ of 32 = _____

3. $\frac{1}{8}$ of 144 = _____

4. $\frac{1}{8}$ of 288 = _____

5. $\frac{1}{8}$ of 232 = _____

6. $\frac{1}{2}$ of 98 = _____

7. $\frac{1}{2}$ of 42 = _____

8. $\frac{1}{2}$ of 178 = _____

9. $\frac{1}{2}$ of 214 = _____

10. $\frac{1}{2}$ of 308 = _____

11. $\frac{7}{10}$ of 100 = _____

12. $\frac{7}{10}$ of 270 = _____

13. $\frac{7}{10}$ of 350 = _____

14. $\frac{7}{10}$ of 420 = _____

15. $\frac{7}{10}$ of 530 = _____

16. $12\frac{1}{2}$% of 80 = _____

17. $12\frac{1}{2}$% of 32 = _____

18. $12\frac{1}{2}$% of 144 = _____

19. $12\frac{1}{2}$% of 288 = _____

20. $12\frac{1}{2}$% of 232 = _____

21. 50% of 98 = _____

22. 50% of 42 = _____

23. 50% of 178 = _____

24. 50% of 214 = _____

25. 50% of 308 = _____

26. 70% of 100 = _____

27. 70% of 270 = _____

28. 70% of 350 = _____

29. 70% of 420 = _____

30. 70% of 530 = _____

Fractional Part of a Number / Finding Percentages

Complete each of the following.

1. $\frac{9}{5}$ of 25 = _____45_____

2. $\frac{9}{5}$ of 40 = _____

3. $\frac{9}{5}$ of 110 = _____

4. $\frac{9}{5}$ of 75 = _____

5. $\frac{9}{5}$ of 150 = _____

6. 180% of 25 = _____

7. 180% of 40 = _____

8. 180% of 110 = _____

9. 180% of 75 = _____

10. 180% of 150 = _____

Find each percentage.

11. 72% of 44 = _____31.68_____

12. 57% of 53 = _____

13. 44% of 72 = _____

14. 127% of 38 = _____

15. 68% of 68 = _____

16. 81% of 68 = _____

17. 62% of 38 = _____

18. 29% of 86 = _____

19. 57% of 36 = _____

20. 38% of 116 = _____

Fractional Part of a Number / Finding Percentages

Complete each of the following.

1. $\frac{4}{5}$ of 35 = _____28_____

2. $\frac{4}{5}$ of 75 = _____

3. $\frac{4}{5}$ of 60 = _____

4. $\frac{4}{5}$ of 105 = _____

5. $\frac{4}{5}$ of 225 = _____

6. $\frac{5}{8}$ of 64 = _____

7. $\frac{5}{8}$ of 80 = _____

8. $\frac{5}{8}$ of 120 = _____

9. $\frac{5}{8}$ of 72 = _____

10. $\frac{5}{8}$ of 248 = _____

11. $\frac{9}{10}$ of 100 = _____

12. $\frac{9}{10}$ of 50 = _____

13. $\frac{9}{10}$ of 140 = _____

14. $\frac{9}{10}$ of 230 = _____

15. $\frac{9}{10}$ of 350 = _____

16. 80% of 35 = _____

17. 80% of 75 = _____

18. 80% of 60 = _____

19. 80% of 105 = _____

20. 80% of 225 = _____

21. $62\frac{1}{2}$% of 64 = _____

22. $62\frac{1}{2}$% of 80 = _____

23. $62\frac{1}{2}$% of 120 = _____

24. $62\frac{1}{2}$% of 72 = _____

25. $62\frac{1}{2}$% of 248 = _____

26. 90% of 100 = _____

27. 90% of 50 = _____

28. 90% of 140 = _____

29. 90% of 230 = _____

30. 90% of 350 = _____

Fractional Part of a Number / Finding Percentages

Complete each of the following.

1. $\frac{7}{4}$ of 16 = _____28_____

2. $\frac{7}{4}$ of 72 = _____

3. $\frac{7}{4}$ of 148 = _____

4. $\frac{7}{4}$ of 116 = _____

5. $\frac{7}{4}$ of 232 = _____

6. 175% of 16 = _____

7. 175% of 72 = _____

8. 175% of 148 = _____

9. 175% of 116 = _____

10. 175% of 232 = _____

Find each percentage.

11. 32% of 61 = _____19.52_____

12. 53% of 78 = _____

13. 126% of 37 = _____

14. 74% of 21 = _____

15. 146% of 37 = _____

16. 15% of 198 = _____

17. 73% of 28 = _____

18. 44% of 92 = _____

19. 23% of 192 = _____

20. 184% of 28 = _____

Common Fraction-to-Percent Equivalences / Finding Percentages

Rewrite each fraction as a percent.

1. $\frac{1}{2}$ = _50_ %   6. $\frac{1}{5}$ = _____ %   11. $\frac{1}{8}$ = _____ %   16. $\frac{7}{10}$ = _____ %

2. $\frac{1}{3}$ = _____ %   7. $\frac{2}{5}$ = _____ %   12. $\frac{3}{8}$ = _____ %   17. $\frac{3}{10}$ = _____ %

3. $\frac{2}{3}$ = _____ %   8. $\frac{3}{5}$ = _____ %   13. $\frac{5}{8}$ = _____ %   18. $\frac{9}{10}$ = _____ %

4. $\frac{1}{4}$ = _____ %   9. $\frac{4}{5}$ = _____ %   14. $\frac{7}{8}$ = _____ %   19. $\frac{5}{4}$ = _____ %

5. $\frac{3}{4}$ = _____ %   10. $\frac{7}{5}$ = _____ %   15. $\frac{9}{8}$ = _____ %   20. $\frac{11}{8}$ = _____ %

Find each percentage.

21. 50% of 20 = ____10____   29. 125% of 72 = _____

22. 75% of 40 = _____   30. 40% of 55 = _____

23. 140% of 35 = _____   31. 75% of 32 = _____

24. $37\frac{1}{2}$% of 96 = _____   32. $33\frac{1}{3}$% of 60 = _____

25. 30% of 200 = _____   33. 90% of 120 = _____

26. 25% of 20 = _____   34. $137\frac{1}{2}$% of 112 = _____

27. 60% of 15 = _____   35. $87\frac{1}{2}$% of 56 = _____

28. $12\frac{1}{2}$% of 64 = _____   36. $166\frac{2}{3}$% of 321 = _____

Rewriting Percents as Decimals / Finding Percentages

Rewrite each percent in decimal form.

1. 48% = _0.48_   6. 17% = _____   11. 167% = _____   16. 250% = _____

2. 92% = _____   7. 87% = _____   12. 105% = _____   17. 700% = _____

3. 56% = _____   8. 42% = _____   13. 110% = _____   18. 1% = _____

4. 12% = _____   9. 31% = _____   14. 0.7% = _____   19. 17.5% = _____

5. 59% = _____   10. 125% = _____   15. 3% = _____   20. 9.3% = _____

Find each percentage.

21. 48% of 29 = ____13.92____   29. 125% of 92 = _____

22. 92% of 76 = _____   30. 250% of 13 = _____

23. 12% of 93 = _____   31. 167% of 42 = _____

24. 59% of 87 = _____   32. 105% of 27 = _____

25. 105% of 46 = _____   33. 0.7% of 324 = _____

26. 17% of 35 = _____   34. 1% of 512 = _____

27. 87% of 43 = _____   35. 17.5% of 22 = _____

28. 31% of 75 = _____   36. 2.8% of 315 = _____

Basic Computation Series 2000: Working with Percents
SECTION 1 Decimals, Fractions, and Percents

Common Fraction-to-Percent Equivalences / Finding Percentages

Rewrite each fraction as a percent.

1. $\frac{5}{8}$ = _$62\frac{1}{2}$_ % 6. $\frac{2}{3}$ = _____ % 11. $\frac{3}{4}$ = _____ % 16. $\frac{9}{5}$ = _____ %

2. $\frac{1}{3}$ = _____ % 7. $\frac{5}{4}$ = _____ % 12. $\frac{7}{8}$ = _____ % 17. $\frac{9}{10}$ = _____ %

3. $\frac{1}{4}$ = _____ % 8. $\frac{3}{8}$ = _____ % 13. $\frac{13}{8}$ = _____ % 18. $\frac{3}{5}$ = _____ %

4. $\frac{11}{8}$ = _____ % 9. $\frac{15}{4}$ = _____ % 14. $\frac{7}{10}$ = _____ % 19. $\frac{5}{3}$ = _____ %

5. $\frac{4}{5}$ = _____ % 10. $\frac{17}{5}$ = _____ % 15. $\frac{2}{9}$ = _____ % 20. $\frac{3}{10}$ = _____ %

Find each percentage.

21. 40% of 95 = _____38_____   29. $62\frac{1}{2}$% of 80 = _____

22. 20% of 425 = _____   30. 25% of 224 = _____

23. $37\frac{1}{2}$% of 216 = _____   31. 70% of 320 = _____

24. 340% of 75 = _____   32. 90% of 110 = _____

25. 140% of 105 = _____   33. $166\frac{2}{3}$% of 63 = _____

26. 25% of 196 = _____   34. 75% of 236 = _____

27. 80% of 265 = _____   35. $66\frac{2}{3}$% of 108 = _____

28. $22\frac{2}{9}$% of 81 = _____   36. $87\frac{1}{2}$% of 184 = _____

Rewriting Percents as Decimals / Finding Percentages

Rewrite each percent in decimal form.

1. 36% = _0.36_   6. 31% = _____   11. 27% = _____   16. 8.2% = _____

2. 57% = _____   7. 19% = _____   12. 5.4% = _____   17. 17.4% = _____

3. 46% = _____   8. 16% = _____   13. 3.7% = _____   18. 13.6% = _____

4. 8% = _____   9. 23% = _____   14. 8.1% = _____   19. 15.9% = _____

5. 13% = _____   10. 132% = _____   15. 16.3% = _____   20. 28.1% = _____

Find each percentage.

21. 36% of 43 = _____15.48_____   29. 8.1% of 26 = _____

22. 57% of 28 = _____   30. 3.7% of 48 = _____

23. 46% of 32 = _____   31. 8.2% of 27 = _____

24. 13% of 143 = _____   32. 5.4% of 63 = _____

25. 16% of 86 = _____   33. 13.6% of 67 = _____

26. 31% of 29 = _____   34. 15.9% of 54 = _____

27. 19% of 75 = _____   35. 28.1% of 92 = _____

28. 132% of 49 = _____   36. 1.8% of 110 = _____

Basic Computation Series 2000: Working with Percents
SECTION 1 Decimals, Fractions, and Percents

Common Fraction-to-Percent Equivalences / Finding Percentages

Rewrite each fraction as a percent.

1. $\dfrac{3}{8}$ = $37\frac{1}{2}$ %   6. $\dfrac{3}{5}$ = _____ %   11. $\dfrac{11}{8}$ = _____ %   16. $\dfrac{1}{5}$ = _____ %

2. $\dfrac{5}{4}$ = _____ %   7. $\dfrac{7}{8}$ = _____ %   12. $\dfrac{1}{2}$ = _____ %   17. $\dfrac{3}{10}$ = _____ %

3. $\dfrac{8}{5}$ = _____ %   8. $\dfrac{1}{4}$ = _____ %   13. $\dfrac{2}{5}$ = _____ %   18. $\dfrac{5}{3}$ = _____ %

4. $\dfrac{1}{3}$ = _____ %   9. $\dfrac{2}{3}$ = _____ %   14. $\dfrac{5}{8}$ = _____ %   19. $\dfrac{3}{4}$ = _____ %

5. $\dfrac{13}{4}$ = _____ %   10. $\dfrac{7}{10}$ = _____ %   15. $\dfrac{4}{5}$ = _____ %   20. $\dfrac{5}{9}$ = _____ %

Find each percentage.

21. 70% of 130 = 91 29. 175% of 56 = _____

22. $137\frac{1}{2}$% of 40 = _____   30. 80% of 135 = _____

23. 50% of 162 = _____   31. $33\frac{1}{3}$% of 93 = _____

24. 40% of 95 = _____   32. 125% of 64 = _____

25. $62\frac{1}{2}$% of 96 = _____   33. 160% of 105 = _____

26. $87\frac{1}{2}$% of 128 = _____   34. 60% of 125 = _____

27. 20% of 40 = _____   35. $166\frac{2}{3}$% of 81 = _____

28. $37\frac{1}{2}$% of 88 = _____   36. $12\frac{1}{2}$% of 328 = _____

Rewriting Percents as Decimals / Finding Percentages

Rewrite each percent in decimal form.

1. 26% = _0.26_

2. 5% = _____

3. 16% = _____

4. 82% = _____

5. 8% = _____

6. 12% = _____

7. 29% = _____

8. 32% = _____

9. 9% = _____

10. 17% = _____

11. 6.9% = _____

12. 7.62% = _____

13. 0.31% = _____

14. 810% = _____

15. 9.6% = _____

16. 3.2% = _____

17. 5.14% = _____

18. 0.23% = _____

19. 0.3% = _____

20. 114% = _____

Find each percentage.

21. 26% of 87 = ___22.62___

22. 16% of 96 = _____

23. 82% of 16 = _____

24. 8% of 503 = _____

25. 810% of 43 = _____

26. 12% of 67 = _____

27. 29% of 56 = _____

28. 32% of 82 = _____

29. 9% of 243 = _____

30. 17% of 106 = _____

31. 3.2% of 69 = _____

32. 5.14% of 73 = _____

33. 0.23% of 53 = _____

34. 0.3% of 2,731 = _____

35. 114% of 29 = _____

36. 0.03% of 804 = _____

Basic Computation Series 2000: Working with Percents
SECTION 1 Decimals, Fractions, and Percents

Common Fraction-to-Percent Equivalences / Finding Percentages

Rewrite each fraction as a percent.

1. $\frac{9}{10} = \underline{\quad 90 \quad}$ %   **6.** $\frac{9}{4} = \underline{\qquad}$ %   **11.** $\frac{2}{5} = \underline{\qquad}$ %   **16.** $\frac{7}{5} = \underline{\qquad}$ %

2. $\frac{1}{8} = \underline{\qquad}$ %   **7.** $\frac{1}{4} = \underline{\qquad}$ %   **12.** $\frac{17}{8} = \underline{\qquad}$ %   **17.** $\frac{15}{8} = \underline{\qquad}$ %

3. $\frac{13}{10} = \underline{\qquad}$ %   **8.** $\frac{3}{4} = \underline{\qquad}$ %   **13.** $\frac{5}{8} = \underline{\qquad}$ %   **18.** $\frac{1}{2} = \underline{\qquad}$ %

4. $\frac{5}{4} = \underline{\qquad}$ %   **9.** $\frac{3}{8} = \underline{\qquad}$ %   **14.** $\frac{13}{4} = \underline{\qquad}$ %   **19.** $\frac{9}{5} = \underline{\qquad}$ %

5. $\frac{1}{9} = \underline{\qquad}$ %   **10.** $\frac{7}{8} = \underline{\qquad}$ %   **15.** $\frac{7}{10} = \underline{\qquad}$ %   **20.** $\frac{11}{9} = \underline{\qquad}$ %

Find each percentage.

21. $37\frac{1}{2}$% of 16 = $\underline{\qquad 6 \qquad}$ **29.** $12\frac{1}{2}$% of 88 = $\underline{\qquad}$

22. 75% of 48 = $\underline{\qquad}$ **30.** 25% of 188 = $\underline{\qquad}$

23. 70% of 30 = $\underline{\qquad}$ **31.** 75% of 204 = $\underline{\qquad}$

24. $87\frac{1}{2}$% of 32 = $\underline{\qquad}$ **32.** 225% of 92 = $\underline{\qquad}$

25. 50% of 150 = $\underline{\qquad}$ **33.** 130% of 150 = $\underline{\qquad}$

26. $122\frac{2}{9}$% of 18 = $\underline{\qquad}$ **34.** $11\frac{1}{9}$% of 63 = $\underline{\qquad}$

27. 90% of 140 = $\underline{\qquad}$ **35.** 125% of 124 = $\underline{\qquad}$

28. 180% of 65 = $\underline{\qquad}$ **36.** $166\frac{2}{3}$% of 321 = $\underline{\qquad}$

Rewriting Percents as Decimals / Finding Percentages

Rewrite each percent in decimal form.

1. 22% = _0.22_

2. 13% = _____

3. 72% = _____

4. 81% = _____

5. 24% = _____

6. 69% = _____

7. 52% = _____

8. 55% = _____

9. 32% = _____

10. 137% = _____

11. 17.2% = _____

12. 18.1% = _____

13. 5.3% = _____

14. 113% = _____

15. 15.1% = _____

16. 9.2% = _____

17. 0.35% = _____

18. 1.4% = _____

19. 9.5% = _____

20. 8.1% = _____

Find each percentage.

21. 22% of 81 = _17.82_

22. 13% of 65 = _____

23. 52% of 19 = _____

24. 81% of 63 = _____

25. 24% of 60 = _____

26. 72% of 17 = _____

27. 32% of 63 = _____

28. 17.2% of 32 = _____

29. 18.1% of 15 = _____

30. 0.3% of 98 = _____

31. 15.1% of 76 = _____

32. 9.2% of 57 = _____

33. 0.35% of 600 = _____

34. 1.4% of 28 = _____

35. 113% of 56 = _____

36. 17.3% of 67 = _____

Common Fraction-to-Percent Equivalences / Finding Percentages

Rewrite each fraction as a percent.

1. $\frac{2}{5}$ = _40_ %   **6.** $\frac{5}{3}$ = _____ %   **11.** $\frac{4}{5}$ = _____ %   **16.** $\frac{3}{10}$ = _____ %

2. $\frac{2}{3}$ = _____ %   **7.** $\frac{3}{8}$ = _____ %   **12.** $\frac{1}{3}$ = _____ %   **17.** $\frac{7}{4}$ = _____ %

3. $\frac{5}{4}$ = _____ %   **8.** $\frac{3}{2}$ = _____ %   **13.** $\frac{1}{2}$ = _____ %   **18.** $\frac{7}{3}$ = _____ %

4. $\frac{7}{5}$ = _____ %   **9.** $\frac{3}{5}$ = _____ %   **14.** $\frac{1}{8}$ = _____ %   **19.** $\frac{1}{9}$ = _____ %

5. $\frac{7}{10}$ = _____ %   **10.** $\frac{3}{4}$ = _____ %   **15.** $\frac{1}{5}$ = _____ %   **20.** $\frac{13}{10}$ = _____ %

Find each percentage.

21. 125% of 36 = _____45_____   **29.** 140% of 85 = _____

22. 70% of 90 = _____   **30.** $37\frac{1}{2}$% of 32 = _____

23. $166\frac{2}{3}$% of 81 = _____   **31.** 75% of 108 = _____

24. 30% of 110 = _____   **32.** 175% of 92 = _____

25. 130% of 50 = _____   **33.** $66\frac{2}{3}$% of 54 = _____

26. 80% of 65 = _____   **34.** $11\frac{1}{9}$% of 90 = _____

27. 40% of 125 = _____   **35.** $33\frac{1}{3}$% of 66 = _____

28. 150% of 90 = _____   **36.** 125% of 36 = _____

Rewriting Percents as Decimals / Finding Percentages

Rewrite each percent in decimal form.

1. 42% = _0.42_   6. 83% = _____   11. 12.2% = _____   16. 3.5% = _____

2. 35% = _____   7. 9% = _____   12. 8.7% = _____   17. 12.9% = _____

3. 58% = _____   8. 72% = _____   13. 115% = _____   18. 5.2% = _____

4. 7% = _____   9. 77% = _____   14. 0.32% = _____   19. 14.1% = _____

5. 16% = _____   10. 89% = _____   15. 6.9% = _____   20. 0.03% = _____

Find each percentage.

21. 42% of 94 = _39.48_   29. 8.7% of 335 = _____

22. 35% of 27 = _____   30. 115% of 27 = _____

23. 58% of 63 = _____   31. 0.32% of 93 = _____

24. 77% of 217 = _____   32. 6.9% of 102 = _____

25. 16% of 405 = _____   33. 3.5% of 61 = _____

26. 9% of 376 = _____   34. 12.9% of 53 = _____

27. 7% of 931 = _____   35. 14.1% of 57 = _____

28. 12.2% of 76 = _____   36. 2.3% of 15 = _____

Basic Computation Series 2000: Working with Percents
SECTION 1 Decimals, Fractions, and Percents

Finding Percentages

Find each percentage.

1. 12% of 32 = _____3.84_____

11. 75% of 128 = _____

2. 25% of 76 = _____

12. 15.2% of 7.3 = _____

3. 13% of 93 = _____

13. 30% of 150 = _____

4. 20% of 85 = _____

14. 28.2% of 36 = _____

5. 37% of 83 = _____

15. 50% of 86 = _____

6. 10% of 110 = _____

16. 17.5% of 7.2 = _____

7. 6.1% of 121 = _____

17. 90% of 380 = _____

8. 60% of 95 = _____

18. 63.2% of 99 = _____

9. 12.3% of 69 = _____

19. 40% of 275 = _____

10. 80% of 155 = _____

20. 8.7% of 68 = _____

Sales Tax

The sales tax charged in a certain county is 8%. For each of the following purchases, find the amount of sales tax charged on the purchase and the total cost of the purchase. Round each answer to the nearest cent.

Purchase	Sales Tax	Total	Purchase	Sales Tax	Total
1. $28.70	$2.30	$31.00	11. $105.14		
2. $56.10			12. $67.30		
3. $45.11			13. $55.21		
4. $63.19			14. $76.13		
5. $27.22			15. $111.10		
6. $93.40			16. $28.32		
7. $67.20			17. $57.30		
8. $100.00			18. $92.13		
9. $75.16			19. $13.56		
10. $88.20			20. $25.90		

Basic Computation Series 2000: Working with Percents
SECTION 1 Decimals, Fractions, and Percents

Finding Percentages

Find each percentage.

1. 17% of 28 = _____4.76_____

2. 8% of 627 = _____

3. 10% of 230 = _____

4. 14.3% of 97 = _____

5. 5.6% of 32 = _____

6. 25% of 112 = _____

7. 9.9% of 76 = _____

8. 12% of 322 = _____

9. 50% of 144 = _____

10. 6% of 1,365 = _____

11. 75% of 384 = _____

12. 19.3% of 63 = _____

13. 27% of 115 = _____

14. 50% of 562 = _____

15. 16% of 76 = _____

16. 39% of 58 = _____

17. 80% of 325 = _____

18. 67% of 83 = _____

19. 53.1% of 93 = _____

20. 17.4% of 67 = _____

Sales Tax

The sales tax charged in a certain county is 7.5%. For each of the following purchases, find the amount of sales tax charged on the purchase and the total cost of the purchase. Round each answer to the nearest cent.

Purchase	Sales Tax	Total
1. $29.36	$2.20	$31.56
2. $87.50		
3. $235.16		
4. $75.52		
5. $93.40		
6. $55.33		
7. $77.36		
8. $92.43		
9. $43.56		
10. $27.38		

Purchase	Sales Tax	Total
11. $50.40		
12. $107.29		
13. $66.95		
14. $98.42		
15. $77.31		
16. $145.20		
17. $88.10		
18. $25.00		
19. $42.95		
20. $66.89		

Finding Percentages

Find each percentage.

1. 13% of 861 = _____111.93_____

2. 50% of 32,876 = _____

3. 27% of 693 = _____

4. 10% of 630 = _____

5. 123% of 76 = _____

6. 90% of 980 = _____

7. 42% of 93 = _____

8. 80% of 435 = _____

9. 7.6% of 32 = _____

10. 30% of 5,630 = _____

11. 8.3% of 67 = _____

12. 25% of 396 = _____

13. 112% of 13 = _____

14. 12.5% of 64 = _____

15. 56% of 163 = _____

16. 75% of 444 = _____

17. 42% of 94 = _____

18. 70% of 1,220 = _____

19. 60% of 555 = _____

20. 76% of 23 = _____

Sales Tax

The sales tax charged in a certain county is 8.5%. For each of the following purchases, find the amount of sales tax charged on the purchase and the total cost of the purchase. Round each answer to the nearest cent.

Purchase	Sales Tax	Total
1. $29.90	$2.54	$32.44
2. $167.30		
3. $52.37		
4. $98.21		
5. $262.35		
6. $72.95		
7. $85.40		
8. $37.55		
9. $10.10		
10. $42.37		

Purchase	Sales Tax	Total
11. $29.15		
12. $67.14		
13. $106.49		
14. $77.51		
15. $67.30		
16. $55.22		
17. $108.32		
18. $29.56		
19. $76.33		
20. $300.00		

Basic Computation Series 2000: Working with Percents
SECTION 1 Decimals, Fractions, and Percents

Finding Percentages

Find each percentage.

1. 13.2% of 83 = ___*10.956*___

2. 10% of 830 = _____

3. 15% of 1,640 = _____

4. 50% of 1,550 = _____

5. 7% of 1,382 = _____

6. 23.1% of 680 = _____

7. 126% of 32 = _____

8. 75% of 3,004 = _____

9. 59% of 692 = _____

10. 30% of 670 = _____

11. $66\frac{2}{3}$% of 69 = _____

12. 25% of 3,984 = _____

13. 7.8% of 64 = _____

14. 60% of 375 = _____

15. 12.5% of 96 = _____

16. 23.3% of 11 = _____

17. 80% of 625 = _____

18. 66% of 58 = _____

19. 40% of 835 = _____

20. $33\frac{1}{3}$% of 54 = _____

Sales Tax

The sales tax charged in a certain county is 5.5%. For each of the following purchases, find the amount of sales tax charged on the purchase and the total cost of the purchase. Round each answer to the nearest cent.

Purchase	Sales Tax	Total	Purchase	Sales Tax	Total
1. $48.32	$2.66	$50.98	11. $87.40		
2. $27.30			12. $63.51		
3. $68.95			13. $77.20		
4. $99.50			14. $154.32		
5. $182.37			15. $90.25		
6. $72.31			16. $47.47		
7. $90.36			17. $92.19		
8. $252.33			18. $75.28		
9. $76.91			19. $66.81		
10. $88.50			20. $32.11		

Finding Percentages

Find each percentage.

1. 27% of 133 = _____ 35.91 _____

2. 75% of 1,324 = _____

3. 16.2% of 41 = _____

4. 10% of 46,320 = _____

5. 123% of 72 = _____

6. 25% of 1,684 = _____

7. 4.3% of 67 = _____

8. 5.4% of 32 = _____

9. 60% of 905 = _____

10. 67% of 302 = _____

11. 80% of 665 = _____

12. 65% of 38 = _____

13. $33\frac{1}{3}$% of 99 = _____

14. $12\frac{1}{2}$% of 128 = _____

15. 54% of 381 = _____

16. $66\frac{2}{3}$% of 333 = _____

17. 77% of 62 = _____

18. 50% of 1,000 = _____

19. 38.1% of 53 = _____

20. 70% of 830 = _____

Sales Tax

The sales tax charged in a certain county is 7%. For each of the following purchases, find the amount of sales tax charged on the purchase and the total cost of the purchase. Round each answer to the nearest cent.

Purchase	Sales Tax	Total	Purchase	Sales Tax	Total
1. $5.35	$0.37	$5.72	**11.** $86.00		
2. $17.50			**12.** $37.50		
3. $55.25			**13.** $29.30		
4. $36.49			**14.** $55.25		
5. $82.21			**15.** $104.00		
6. $105.16			**16.** $92.92		
7. $27.92			**17.** $69.50		
8. $106.14			**18.** $77.55		
9. $35.42			**19.** $38.22		
10. $88.17			**20.** $72.11		

Rates, Bases, and Percentages

As evidenced by examples in Section 1, percents are most often used to find a percentage of a particular number. To calculate percentage, the following equation can be used:

base × rate = percentage

In this equation, the *base* is the given number, the *rate* is the percent written as a fraction or as a decimal, and the *percentage* is the product, the result of the multiplication.

The relationship between multiplication and division can be used to transform an equation such as 3 × 2 = 6 to either 6 ÷ 2 = 3 or 6 ÷ 3 = 2. In the same way, the equation above can be rewritten in two ways:

base = percentage ÷ rate   *rate = percentage ÷ base*

The three different forms of this equation can be used to find the missing base, rate, or percentage in many problems involving percents. Study the examples below to learn how to use these equations.

Example 1: 1 is what percent of 4?

Solution: To answer the question "what percent," it is necessary to find the rate. Use the equation *rate = percentage ÷ base*. The percentage is 1 and the base is 4.

$$rate = percentage \div base$$

$$rate = 1 \div 4$$

Method 1: $\frac{1}{4} = 0.25$, which, when written as a percent, is 25%.

Method 2: $\frac{1}{4} = \frac{25}{100}$, which, when written as a percent, is 25%.

Thus, 1 is 25% of 4.

Example 2: 43.68 is 28% of what number?

Solution: To answer the question "what number," it is necessary to find the base. Use the equation *base = percentage ÷ rate*. The percentage is 43.68 and the rate is 28%. Before completing the arithmetic, change the rate to a decimal fraction or a common fraction.

$$base = percentage \div rate$$

$$base = 43.68 \div 0.28$$

43.68 ÷ 0.28 = 156. Thus, 43.68 is 28% of 156.

Example 3: What is 32% of 56?

Solution: To answer the question it is necessary to find a given percent of a certain number. This is the percentage. The rate and base are given. Use the equation *percentage = base × rate*. The base is 56 and the rate is 32%. Before completing the arithmetic, change the rate to a decimal fraction or a common fraction.

$$percentage = base \times rate$$

$$percentage = 56 \times 0.32$$

56 × 0.32 = 17.92. Thus, 32% of 56 = 17.92.

Finding Rates

Find each percent.

1. $\frac{1}{2}$ is what percent? _____50%_____

2. $\frac{3}{5}$ is what percent? _____

3. $\frac{1}{4}$ is what percent? _____

4. $\frac{1}{10}$ is what percent? _____

5. $\frac{4}{5}$ is what percent? _____

6. $\frac{3}{4}$ is what percent? _____

7. $\frac{3}{10}$ is what percent? _____

8. $\frac{5}{8}$ is what percent? _____

9. $\frac{2}{5}$ is what percent? _____

10. $\frac{7}{8}$ is what percent? _____

11. 4 is what percent of 5? _____

12. 7 is what percent of 10? _____

13. 1 is what percent of 2? _____

14. 3 is what percent of 4? _____

15. 5 is what percent of 8? _____

16. 2 is what percent of 5? _____

17. 3 is what percent of 10? _____

18. 1 is what percent of 4? _____

19. 3 is what percent of 5? _____

20. 6 is what percent of 12? _____

Finding Bases

Solve each problem.

1. 11.61 is 43% of what number? 27	**7.** 12.88 is 92% of what number?
2. 11 is 25% of what number?	**8.** 1.61 is 23% of what number?
3. 50.96 is 91% of what number?	**9.** 23.49 is 29% of what number?
4. 30.456 is 42.3% of what number?	**10.** 12.75 is 75% of what number?
5. 21.06 is 26% of what number?	**11.** 21.825 is 29.1% of what number?
6. 40.376 is 72.1% of what number?	**12.** 24.624 is 43.2% of what number?

Basic Computation Series 2000: Working with Percents
SECTION 2 Rates, Bases, and Percentages

Finding Rates

Find each percent.

1. $\frac{1}{3}$ is what percent? $33\frac{1}{3}\%$

2. $\frac{3}{4}$ is what percent? _____

3. $\frac{3}{8}$ is what percent? _____

4. $\frac{3}{5}$ is what percent? _____

5. $\frac{1}{2}$ is what percent? _____

6. $\frac{4}{5}$ is what percent? _____

7. $\frac{2}{3}$ is what percent? _____

8. $\frac{5}{8}$ is what percent? _____

9. $\frac{1}{4}$ is what percent? _____

10. $\frac{7}{10}$ is what percent? _____

11. 3 is what percent of 5? _____

12. 5 is what percent of 8? _____

13. 9 is what percent of 10? _____

14. 1 is what percent of 2? _____

15. 1 is what percent of 4? _____

16. 7 is what percent of 10? _____

17. 3 is what percent of 4? _____

18. 3 is what percent of 8? _____

19. 3 is what percent of 10? _____

20. 2 is what percent of 5? _____

Finding Bases

Solve each problem.

1. 11.76 is 21% of what number? *56*	**7.** 15.96 is 28% of what number?
2. 11.136 is 38.4% of what number?	**8.** 51.3 is 90% of what number?
3. 10.72 is 67% of what number?	**9.** 22.1 is 26% of what number?
4. 51.336 is 55.2% of what number?	**10.** 8.775 is 32.5% of what number?
5. 0.0204 is 0.04% of what number?	**11.** 77.76 is 81% of what number?
6. 8.06 is 26% of what number?	**12.** 21.42 is 42% of what number?

Finding Rates

Find each percent.

1. $\frac{9}{10}$ is what percent? _____90%_____

2. $\frac{5}{8}$ is what percent? _____

3. $\frac{2}{3}$ is what percent? _____

4. $\frac{3}{5}$ is what percent? _____

5. $\frac{1}{2}$ is what percent? _____

6. $\frac{1}{3}$ is what percent? _____

7. $\frac{3}{8}$ is what percent? _____

8. $\frac{3}{4}$ is what percent? _____

9. $\frac{3}{20}$ is what percent? _____

10. $\frac{7}{12}$ is what percent? _____

11. 8 is what percent of 10? _____

12. 4 is what percent of 10? _____

13. 9 is what percent of 10? _____

14. 11 is what percent of 10? _____

15. 5 is what percent of 10? _____

16. 15 is what percent of 10? _____

17. 6 is what percent of 10? _____

18. 20 is what percent of 10? _____

19. 3 is what percent of 10? _____

20. 2 is what percent of 10? _____

Finding Bases

Solve each problem.

1. 20.06 is 59% of what number? 34	**7.** 3.36 is 42% of what number?
2. 4.32 is 27% of what number?	**8.** 4 is 25% of what number?
3. 13.8 is 92% of what number?	**9.** 9.86 is 34% of what number?
4. 11.61 is 43% of what number?	**10.** 3.6 is 72% of what number?
5. 74.98 is 81.5% of what number?	**11.** 64.296 is 89.3% of what number?
6. 12.624 is 26.3% of what number?	**12.** 10.08 is 48% of what number?

Basic Computation Series 2000: Working with Percents
SECTION 2 Rates, Bases, and Percentages

Finding Rates

Find each percent.

1. $\frac{3}{5}$ is what percent? ___60%___

2. $\frac{3}{10}$ is what percent? _____

3. $\frac{3}{4}$ is what percent? _____

4. $\frac{1}{3}$ is what percent? _____

5. $\frac{7}{8}$ is what percent? _____

6. $\frac{5}{8}$ is what percent? _____

7. $\frac{2}{7}$ is what percent? _____

8. $\frac{7}{10}$ is what percent? _____

9. $\frac{2}{3}$ is what percent? _____

10. $\frac{9}{10}$ is what percent? _____

11. 7 is what percent of 14? _____

12. 9 is what percent of 3? _____

13. 12 is what percent of 8? _____

14. 6 is what percent of 5? _____

15. 3 is what percent of 4? _____

16. 16 is what percent of 20? _____

17. 1 is what percent of 3? _____

18. 5 is what percent of 15? _____

19. 7 is what percent of 10? _____

20. 5 is what percent of 8? _____

Finding Bases

Solve each problem.

1. 24.84 is 92% of what number? 27	**7.** 14.56 is 28% of what number?
2. 8.45 is 65% of what number?	**8.** 22.32 is 31% of what number?
3. 33.62 is 82% of what number?	**9.** 24.48 is 51% of what number?
4. 15.12 is 27% of what number?	**10.** 9.75 is 75% of what number?
5. 9.936 is 43.2% of what number?	**11.** 48.72 is 87% of what number?
6. 57.618 is 59.4% of what number?	**12.** 46.92 is 92% of what number?

Basic Computation Series 2000: Working with Percents
SECTION 2 Rates, Bases, and Percentages

NAME _____   DATE _____

Finding Rates

Find each percent.

1. $\frac{3}{5}$ is what percent? _____60%_____

2. $\frac{1}{3}$ is what percent? _____

3. $\frac{1}{2}$ is what percent? _____

4. $\frac{5}{8}$ is what percent? _____

5. $\frac{4}{5}$ is what percent? _____

6. $\frac{1}{4}$ is what percent? _____

7. $\frac{2}{3}$ is what percent? _____

8. $\frac{3}{8}$ is what percent? _____

9. $\frac{7}{10}$ is what percent? _____

10. $\frac{7}{20}$ is what percent? _____

11. 9 is what percent of 18? _____

12. 9 is what percent of 27? _____

13. 9 is what percent of 36? _____

14. 4 is what percent of 16? _____

15. 8 is what percent of 16? _____

16. 12 is what percent of 16? _____

17. 3 is what percent of 10? _____

18. 15 is what percent of 10? _____

19. 12 is what percent of 18? _____

20. 11 is what percent of 22? _____

Finding Bases

Solve each problem.

1. 17.1 is 38% of what number? 45	**7.** 6.72 is 42% of what number?
2. 3.944 is 23.2% of what number?	**8.** 15.66 is 29% of what number?
3. 17.1 is 57% of what number?	**9.** 4.32 is 16% of what number?
4. 21.75 is 29% of what number?	**10.** 39.48 is 42% of what number?
5. 36.54 is 63% of what number?	**11.** 28.14 is 67% of what number?
6. 35.7 is 42% of what number?	**12.** 14.45 is 85% of what number?

Basic Computation Series 2000: Working with Percents
SECTION 2 Rates, Bases, and Percentages

Finding Rates, Bases, and Percentages

Complete the following table.

	base	rate (in percent form)	percentage
1.	28	14%	3.92
2.	48	25%	
3.	82	37%	
4.		42%	6.72
5.	45		15
6.		86%	42.14
7.	88	$12\frac{1}{2}$%	
8.	14		4.06
9.	63		33.39
10.		$66\frac{2}{3}$%	80
11.	47	18%	

Finding Rates, Bases, and Percentages

Complete the following table.

	base	rate (in percent form)	percentage
1.	20	25%	5
2.	16	82%	
3.	36		16.92
4.		75%	48
5.	87	63%	
6.	48		13.92
7.		$33\frac{1}{3}\%$	25
8.	88	$37\frac{1}{2}\%$	
9.		26%	15.34
10.		22%	10.12
11.	60	50%	

Basic Computation Series 2000: Working with Percents
SECTION 2 Rates, Bases, and Percentages

Finding Rates, Bases, and Percentages

Complete the following table.

	base	rate (in percent form)	percentage
1.	89	15%	13.35
2.	28	75%	
3.	35	18%	
4.		50%	45
5.	43		26.66
6.		72%	12.96
7.	60	$33\frac{1}{3}\%$	
8.	56		35
9.		43%	36.55
10.	40	87%	
11.	84		56

Basic Computation Series 2000: Working with Percents
SECTION 2 Rates, Bases, and Percentages

Finding Rates, Bases, and Percentages

Complete the following table.

	base	rate (in percent form)	percentage
1.	90	54%	48.6
2.		25%	8
3.	26		12.48
4.	92	50%	
5.		32%	14.72
6.	54	86%	
7.		$12\frac{1}{2}$%	5
8.	63		21
9.	38	72%	
10.		75%	27
11.	56		16.24

Finding Rates, Bases, and Percentages

Complete the following table.

	base	rate (in percent form)	percentage
1.	69	43%	29.67
2.		25%	11
3.	57	36%	
4.	88		66
5.		16%	9.44
6.	38		17.1
7.		$66\frac{2}{3}\%$	16
8.	24	$12\frac{1}{2}\%$	
9.	86	23%	
10.	96		36
11.		48%	24.96

Finding Rates, Bases, and Percentages

Complete the following table.

	base	rate (in percent form)	percentage
1.	97	16%	15.52
2.		87%	107.88
3.	150	50%	
4.		43%	32.68
5.	78		26
6.	57	26%	
7.	15		7.2
8.		$66\frac{2}{3}\%$	60
9.	48	$62\frac{1}{2}\%$	
10.	67		34.84
11.		25%	31

Finding Rates, Bases, and Percentages

Complete the following table.

	base	rate (in percent form)	percentage
1.	60	75%	45
2.		96%	40.32
3.	80	10%	
4.	75		24
5.		20%	10
6.	120		72
7.		96%	46.08
8.	48	25%	
9.	105	28%	
10.	58		21.46
11.		$12\frac{1}{2}\%$	14

Finding Rates, Bases, and Percentages

Complete the following table.

	base	rate (in percent form)	percentage
1.	16	30%	4.8
2.		38%	32.3
3.	12		9
4.		$12\frac{1}{2}\%$	7
5.	88	14%	
6.	88		22
7.	43	17%	
8.		$66\frac{2}{3}\%$	72
9.	29		24.07
10.		17%	8.84
11.	104		78

Basic Computation Series 2000: Working with Percents
SECTION 2 Rates, Bases, and Percentages

Finding Rates, Bases, and Percentages

Complete the following table.

	base	rate (in percent form)	percentage
1.	98	42%	41.16
2.	75		7.5
3.	116	82%	
4.		75%	93
5.	94		30.08
6.		38%	11.02
7.	48	90%	
8.	104		65
9.	43	15%	
10.	82		46.74
11.		25%	33

Finding Rates, Bases, and Percentages

Complete the following table.

	base	rate (in percent form)	percentage
1.	92	57%	52.44
2.	63	14%	
3.		75%	69
4.	56	$62\frac{1}{2}\%$	
5.	38		16.34
6.		$12\frac{1}{2}\%$	13
7.	27	36%	
8.	25		15
9.		25%	18
10.	87		53.07
11.	56	10%	

Applications Involving Percents

Many times, when an item is advertised as being "on sale" or is offered at a discount, the sale or discount is stated as a percent. In these situations, it is important to be able to determine the amount of money saved on the purchase, and the sale price.

Example 1: A store is offering a 10% discount on a compact disc that ordinarily sells for $25.00. How much is the savings and what is the sale price?

Solution: To find the savings (10% of $25.00), change 10% to a decimal or common fraction and multiply by 25.

$$0.10 \times 25 = 2.5$$

Thus, the savings is $2.50.

To find the sale price, subtract the savings from the original price.

$$25 - 2.50 = 22.50$$

Thus, the sale price is $22.50.

When an item is offered on sale and the sale price is given, it is helpful to know the percent saved.

Example 2: **SAVE ON TAPE RECORDERS**

REGULAR PRICE: $125.00   NOW: $85.49

Given the information above, complete the following table. Round the percent to the nearest hundredth.

item	regular price	sale price	amount saved	percent saved

Solution: 1. Write the name of the item in the appropriate space.

2. Write the regular price in the appropriate space.

3. Write the sale price in the appropriate space.

4. Subtract the sale price from the regular price to find the amount saved.

$$125.00 - 85.49 = 39.51$$

Write $39.51 in the appropriate space.

5. The amount saved is the percentage, the regular price is the base, and the percent saved is the rate. Since *rate = percentage ÷ base*, divide the savings by the regular price to find the percent saved.

$$39.51 \div 125.00 = 0.31608$$

When written as a percent rounded to the nearest hundredth, 0.31608 is 31.61%. Write this number in the appropriate space.

item	regular price	sale price	amount saved	percent saved
tape recorder	$125.00	$85.49	$39.51	31.61%

A hotel statement of charges can often be difficult to decipher. Study the example below to learn how a Guest's Statement and Summary are prepared.

Example 3: The statement below represents the charges for a two-night hotel stay. The occupancy tax is 10% and the sales tax is 8%. Complete the Guest's Statement and the Summary on the following page.

GUEST'S STATEMENT

Date	Reference	Description	Amount	Balance
12/10	RMCH	Room charge	$79.50	
12/10	TAX1	Occupancy tax		
12/10	TAX2	Sales tax		
12/10	FOOD	Restaurant	$37.45	
12/11	RMCH	Room charge	$79.50	
12/11	TAX1	Occupancy tax		
12/11	TAX2	Sales tax		
12/11	FOOD	Restaurant	$48.50	
12/11	TEL	Telephone call	$ 0.75	

Basic Computation Series 2000: Working with Percents
SECTION 3 Applications Involving Percents

SUMMARY

Description	No. of entries	Cost/entry	Total
Room charge			
Occupancy tax			
Sales tax			
Restaurant		—	
Telephone			
TOTALS	—	—	

Solution: A hotel bill is usually written in such form as to show a "running total," or balance, after each charge. Since this type of bill can be confusing to the guest, a summary can be prepared to help clarify the bill. The hotel does not usually provide this service.

To determine the occupancy tax, change 10% to a decimal and multiply by the daily rate. $0.10 \times 79.50 = 7.95$. Thus, the daily occupancy tax is $7.95. To determine the sales tax, change 8% to a decimal and multiply by the daily rate. $0.08 \times 79.50 = 6.36$. Thus, the daily sales tax is $6.36. Write these numbers in the table and calculate the balance after each entry.

GUEST'S STATEMENT

Date	Reference	Description	Amount	Balance
12/10	RMCH	Room charge	$79.50	$ 79.50
12/10	TAX1	Occupancy tax	$ 7.95	$ 87.45
12/10	TAX2	Sales tax	$ 6.36	$ 93.81
12/10	FOOD	Restaurant	$37.45	$131.26
12/11	RMCH	Room charge	$79.50	$210.76
12/11	TAX1	Occupancy tax	$ 7.95	$218.71
12/11	TAX2	Sales tax	$ 6.36	$225.07
12/11	FOOD	Restaurant	$48.50	$273.57
12/11	TEL	Telephone call	$ 0.75	$274.32

Next, complete the summary as shown below. This provides a check on the work above.

SUMMARY

Description	No. of entries	Cost/entry	Total
Room charge	2	$79.50	$159.00
Occupancy tax	2	$ 7.95	$ 15.90
Sales tax	2	$ 6.36	$ 12.72
Restaurant	2	—	$ 85.95
Telephone	1	$ 0.75	$ 0.75
TOTALS	—	—	$274.32

The final balance on the Guest's Statement and the final total on the summary are the same. Therefore, the statement is correct.

Discounts

For each item, find the amount saved and the sale price.

1. Item: computer software

Regular Price: $57.78

Discount: 15%

Savings: _____$8.67_____

Sale Price: _____$49.11_____

5. Item: jewelry

Regular Price: $29.98

Discount: 18%

Savings: _____

Sale Price: _____

2. Item: cassette tape player

Regular Price: $38.90

Discount: 10%

Savings: _____

Sale Price: _____

6. Item: hair dryer

Regular Price: $28.50

Discount: 40%

Savings: _____

Sale Price: _____

3. Item: camera

Regular Price: $35.45

Discount: 40%

Savings: _____

Sale Price: _____

7. Item: calculator

Regular Price: $19.75

Discount: 30%

Savings: _____

Sale Price: _____

4. Item: digital watch

Regular Price: $21.96

Discount: 25%

Savings: _____

Sale Price: _____

8. Item: pen/pencil set

Regular Price: $27.50

Discount: 40%

Savings: _____

Sale Price: _____

Discounts

Complete the following table.

	item	regular price	discount	savings	sale price
1.	1 pair slacks	$37.50	20%	$7.50	$30.00
2.	1 blouse	$30.00	$33\frac{1}{3}\%$		
3.	1 swimsuit	$62.50	40%		
4.	1 shirt	$32.50	10%		
5.	1 pair jeans	$42.00	20%		
6.	1 pair shoes	$64.00	$12\frac{1}{2}\%$		
7.	1 pair shorts	$27.00	15%		
8.	1 belt	$18.50	10%		

Basic Computation Series 2000: Working with Percents
SECTION 3 Applications Involving Percents

Discounts

For each item, find the amount saved and the sale price.

1. Item: computer software

Regular Price: $219.95

Discount: 12%

Savings: _$26.39_

Sale Price: _$193.56_

2. Item: cassette tape player

Regular Price: $45.40

Discount: 25%

Savings: _____

Sale Price: _____

3. Item: camera

Regular Price: $21.50

Discount: 30%

Savings: _____

Sale Price: _____

4. Item: digital watch

Regular Price: $28.50

Discount: 20%

Savings: _____

Sale Price: _____

5. Item: jewelry

Regular Price: $198.50

Discount: 22%

Savings: _____

Sale Price: _____

6. Item: hair dryer

Regular Price: $21.50

Discount: 20%

Savings: _____

Sale Price: _____

7. Item: calculator

Regular Price: $26.00

Discount: 15%

Savings: _____

Sale Price: _____

8. Item: pen/pencil set

Regular Price: $27.00

Discount: 30%

Savings: _____

Sale Price: _____

Discounts

Complete the following table.

	item	regular price	discount	savings	sale price
1.	1 pair slacks	$93.30	$33\frac{1}{3}\%$	$31.10	$62.20
2.	1 blouse	$32.40	25%		
3.	1 swimsuit	$48.80	$12\frac{1}{2}\%$		
4.	1 shirt	$42.00	40%		
5.	1 pair jeans	$48.50	20%		
6.	1 pair shoes	$84.50	10%		
7.	1 pair shorts	$63.60	$33\frac{1}{3}\%$		
8.	1 belt	$24.00	$12\frac{1}{2}\%$		

Basic Computation Series 2000: Working with Percents
SECTION 3 Applications Involving Percents

Discounts

For each item, find the amount saved and the sale price.

1. Item: computer software

Regular Price: $38.95

Discount: 26%

Savings: _____$10.13_____

Sale Price: _____$28.82_____

2. Item: cassette tape player

Regular Price: $59.95

Discount: 40%

Savings: _____

Sale Price: _____

3. Item: camera

Regular Price: $28.80

Discount: 25%

Savings: _____

Sale Price: _____

4. Item: digital watch

Regular Price: $25.90

Discount: 30%

Savings: _____

Sale Price: _____

5. Item: jewelry

Regular Price: $159.50

Discount: 21%

Savings: _____

Sale Price: _____

6. Item: hair dryer

Regular Price: $18.80

Discount: 15%

Savings: _____

Sale Price: _____

7. Item: calculator

Regular Price: $19.80

Discount: 10%

Savings: _____

Sale Price: _____

8. Item: pen/pencil set

Regular Price: $32.00

Discount: 25%

Savings: _____

Sale Price: _____

Discounts

Complete the following table.

	item	regular price	discount	savings	sale price
1.	1 pair slacks	$65.80	10%	$6.58	$59.22
2.	1 blouse	$39.00	30%		
3.	1 swimsuit	$40.98	$33\frac{1}{3}$%		
4.	1 shirt	$31.25	40%		
5.	1 pair jeans	$47.36	25%		
6.	1 pair shoes	$77.49	$33\frac{1}{3}$%		
7.	1 pair shorts	$27.25	20%		
8.	1 belt	$23.10	$33\frac{1}{3}$%		

Discounts

For each item, find the amount saved and the sale price.

1. Item: computer software

   Regular Price: $85.50

   Discount: 13%

   Savings: ___$11.12___

   Sale Price: ___$74.38___

2. Item: cassette tape player

   Regular Price: $39.95

   Discount: 20%

   Savings: _____

   Sale Price: _____

3. Item: camera

   Regular Price: $17.50

   Discount: 10%

   Savings: _____

   Sale Price: _____

4. Item: digital watch

   Regular Price: $32.40

   Discount: 25%

   Savings: _____

   Sale Price: _____

5. Item: jewelry

   Regular Price: $150.00

   Discount: 25%

   Savings: _____

   Sale Price: _____

6. Item: hair dryer

   Regular Price: $23.44

   Discount: 25%

   Savings: _____

   Sale Price: _____

7. Item: calculator

   Regular Price: $25.50

   Discount: 20%

   Savings: _____

   Sale Price: _____

8. Item: pen/pencil set

   Regular Price: $26.30

   Discount: 20%

   Savings: _____

   Sale Price: _____

Discounts

Complete the following table.

	item	regular price	discount	savings	sale price
1.	1 pair slacks	$72.25	40%	$28.90	$43.35
2.	1 blouse	$48.75	20%		
3.	1 swimsuit	$63.40	25%		
4.	1 shirt	$29.40	10%		
5.	1 pair jeans	$39.60	15%		
6.	1 pair shoes	$48.60	30%		
7.	1 pair shorts	$27.50	20%		
8.	1 belt	$17.50	20%		

Basic Computation Series 2000: Working with Percents
SECTION 3 Applications Involving Percents

Discounts

For each item, find the amount saved and the sale price.

1. Item: computer software

Regular Price: $217.00

Discount: 15%

Savings: ___$32.55___

Sale Price: ___$184.45___

2. Item: cassette tape player

Regular Price: $49.95

Discount: 20%

Savings: _____

Sale Price: _____

3. Item: camera

Regular Price: $32.00

Discount: 25%

Savings: _____

Sale Price: _____

4. Item: digital watch

Regular Price: $28.50

Discount: 10%

Savings: _____

Sale Price: _____

5. Item: jewelry

Regular Price: $45.00

Discount: 18%

Savings: _____

Sale Price: _____

6. Item: hair dryer

Regular Price: $21.50

Discount: 10%

Savings: _____

Sale Price: _____

7. Item: calculator

Regular Price: $27.44

Discount: 25%

Savings: _____

Sale Price: _____

8. Item: pen/pencil set

Regular Price: $35.00

Discount: 15%

Savings: _____

Sale Price: _____

Discounts

Complete the following table.

item	regular price	discount	savings	sale price
1. 1 pair slacks	$49.50	20%	$9.90	$39.60
2. 1 blouse	$42.20	25%		
3. 1 swimsuit	$38.50	20%		
4. 1 shirt	$29.45	40%		
5. 1 pair jeans	$37.60	15%		
6. 1 pair shoes	$73.50	20%		
7. 1 pair shorts	$28.56	25%		
8. 1 belt	$16.50	10%		

Basic Computation Series 2000: Working with Percents
SECTION 3 Applications Involving Percents

Sales

Complete the table below. Round percents to the nearest hundredth.

Complete Package!!
Computer, Monitor, and Printer
Save Over 30%
Regular price: $1,297.97 Now: $899.97

Sale: Save 10%–50% on Selected Items

flatbed scanner	regular price:	$89.99	NOW:	$59.99
spreadsheet program	regular price:	$59.99	NOW:	$39.99
file crate	regular price:	$5.99	NOW:	$3.99
computer workstation	regular price:	$99.99	NOW:	$79.99
desk chair	regular price:	$169.99	NOW:	$149.99
color jet printer	regular price:	$119.99	NOW:	$89.99

item	regular price	sale price	amount saved	percent saved
1. computer package				
2. flatbed scanner				
3. spreadsheet program				
4. file crate				
5. computer workstation				
6. desk chair				
7. color jet printer				

Hotel Statements

Complete the following Guest's Statement and Summary. The occupancy tax is 10% and the sales tax is 8%.

Good Night's Rest Hotel
999 ZZZ Street   Vacationville, USA
Phone: 1 888 555-3333   FAX: 1 888 555-3331

GUEST'S STATEMENT

Date	Reference	Description	Charge	Balance
4/17	RMCH	Room charge	$79.00	
4/17	TAX1	Occupancy tax		
4/17	TAX2	Sales tax		
4/17	TEL	Telephone call	$ 0.75	
4/17	FOOD	Restaurant	$35.75	
4/18	RMCH	Room charge	$79.00	
4/18	TAX1	Occupancy tax		
4/18	TAX2	Sales tax		
4/18	FOOD	Restaurant	$46.12	
4/19	RMCH	Room charge	$79.00	
4/19	TAX1	Occupancy tax		
4/19	TAX2	Sales tax		

SUMMARY

Description	No. of entries	Cost/entry	Total
Room charge			
Occupancy tax			
Sales tax			
Restaurant		—	
Telephone			
TOTALS	—	—	

Sales

Complete the table below. Round percents to the nearest hundredth.

Sale: Save 10%–50% on Selected Items

35-mm camera	regular price: $109.99	NOW: $79.99
35-mm film	regular price: $5.99	NOW: $3.99
flashlight	regular price: $15.99	NOW: $13.49
flashlight batteries	regular price: $4.59	NOW: $2.99
classic videos	regular price: $17.99	NOW: $15.99
designer watches	regular price: $28.99	NOW: $25.99
CD boombox	regular price: $79.99	NOW: $59.99

item	regular price	sale price	amount saved	percent saved
1. 35-mm camera				
2. 35-mm film				
3. flashlight				
4. flashlight batteries				
5. classic videos				
6. designer watches				
7. CD boombox				

Hotel Statements

Complete the following Guest's Statement and Summary. The occupancy tax is 10% and the sales tax is 8%.

Dream In Peace Hotel
8585 Rest Street   Dreamtown, USA
Phone: 1 888 555-2333   FAX: 1 888 555-2331

GUEST'S STATEMENT

Date	Reference	Description	Charge	Balance
2/11	RMCH	Room charge	$88.50	
2/11	TAX1	Occupancy tax		
2/11	TAX2	Sales tax		
2/11	TEL	Telephone call	$ 0.75	
2/11	FOOD	Restaurant	$27.95	
2/12	RMCH	Room charge	$88.50	
2/12	TAX1	Occupancy tax		
2/12	TAX2	Sales tax		
2/13	RMCH	Room charge	$88.50	
2/13	TAX1	Occupancy tax		
2/13	TAX2	Sales tax		
2/13	FOOD	Restaurant	$57.16	

SUMMARY

Description	No. of entries	Cost/entry	Total
Room charge			
Occupancy tax			
Sales tax			
Restaurant		—	
Telephone			
TOTALS	—	—	

Sales

Complete the table below. Round percents to the nearest hundredth.

Sale: Save 10%–50% on Selected Items

shampoo	regular price:	$3.69	NOW:	$2.50
hair spray	regular price:	$4.59	NOW:	$3.59
toothpaste	regular price:	$5.99	NOW:	$4.99
bath soap	regular price:	$0.89	NOW:	$0.79
face soap	regular price:	$1.29	NOW:	$0.99
fragrance	regular price:	$17.50	NOW:	$13.49
paper towels	regular price:	$1.59	NOW:	$1.29

item	regular price	sale price	amount saved	percent saved
1. shampoo				
2. hair spray				
3. toothpaste				
4. bath soap				
5. face soap				
6. fragrance				
7. paper towels				

Hotel Statements

Complete the following Guest's Statement and Summary. The occupancy tax is 10% and the sales tax is 8%.

Heavenly Hotel
3333 Cloud Street   Heavenly, USA
Phone: 1 888 555-1333   FAX: 1 888 555-1331

GUEST'S STATEMENT

Date	Reference	Description	Charge	Balance
6/10	RMCH	Room charge	$104.00	
6/10	TAX1	Occupancy tax		
6/10	TAX2	Sales tax		
6/10	TEL	Telephone call	$ 0.75	
6/10	FOOD	Restaurant	$ 28.95	
6/11	RMCH	Room charge	$104.00	
6/11	TAX1	Occupancy tax		
6/11	TAX2	Sales tax		
6/11	FOOD	Restaurant	$ 38.60	
6/12	RMCH	Room charge	$104.00	
6/12	TAX1	Occupancy tax		
6/12	TAX2	Sales tax		

SUMMARY

Description	No. of entries	Cost/entry	Total
Room charge			
Occupancy tax			
Sales tax			
Restaurant		—	
Telephone			
TOTALS	—	—	

Sales

Complete the table below. Round percents to the nearest hundredth.

Sale: Save 10%–50% on Selected Items

men and boy's sweaters	regular price: $38.00	NOW: $26.60
men and boy's shirts	regular price: $36.00	NOW: $24.99
men and boy's leather coats	regular price: $260.00	NOW: $129.99
men and boy's corduroy pants	regular price: $45.00	NOW: $39.99
men and boy's jeans	regular price: $54.00	NOW: $39.99
men and boy's running shoes	regular price: $85.00	NOW: $62.99
men and boy's sweatshirts	regular price: $29.00	NOW: $17.40

item	regular price	sale price	amount saved	percent saved
1. sweaters				
2. shirts				
3. leather coats				
4. corduroy pants				
5. jeans				
6. running shoes				
7. sweatshirts				

Hotel Statements

Complete the following Guest's Statement and Summary. The occupancy tax is 10% and the sales tax is 8%.

Buena Vista Hotel
2727 View Street   Seashore, USA
Phone: 1 888 555-9333   FAX: 1 888 555-9331

GUEST'S STATEMENT

Date	Reference	Description	Charge	Balance
10/05	RMCH	Room charge	$62.50	
10/05	TAX1	Occupancy tax		
10/05	TAX2	Sales tax		
10/06	RMCH	Room charge	$62.50	
10/06	TAX1	Occupancy tax		
10/06	TAX2	Sales tax		
10/06	FOOD	Restaurant	$42.45	
10/07	RMCH	Room charge	$62.50	
10/07	TAX1	Occupancy tax		
10/07	TAX2	Sales tax		
10/07	FOOD	Restaurant	$28.49	
10/07	TEL	Telephone call	$ 0.75	

SUMMARY

Description	No. of entries	Cost/entry	Total
Room charge			
Occupancy tax			
Sales tax			
Restaurant		—	
Telephone			
TOTALS	—	—	

Basic Computation Series 2000: Working with Percents
SECTION 3 Applications Involving Percents

Sales

Complete the table below. Round percents to the nearest hundredth.

Sale: Save 10%–50% on Selected Items

women and girl's sweaters	regular price: $42.00	NOW: $24.99
women and girl's casual jackets	regular price: $69.00	NOW: $49.99
women and girl's casual shirts	regular price: $34.99	NOW: $27.99
women and girl's casual slacks	regular price: $38.00	NOW: $32.99
women and girl's jeans	regular price: $29.99	NOW: $23.99
women and girl's boots	regular price: $49.95	NOW: $38.99
women and girl's dress shoes	regular price: $45.95	NOW: $38.50

item	regular price	sale price	amount saved	percent saved
1. sweaters				
2. jackets				
3. shirts				
4. slacks				
5. jeans				
6. boots				
7. dress shoes				

Hotel Statements

Complete the following Guest's Statement and Summary. The occupancy tax is 10% and the sales tax is 8%.

Stay Longer Hotel
2000 Long Street   National, USA
Phone: 1 888 555-4242   FAX: 1 888 555-4241

GUEST'S STATEMENT

Date	Reference	Description	Charge	Balance
4/17	RMCH	Room charge	$88.00	
4/17	TAX1	Occupancy tax		
4/17	TAX2	Sales tax		
4/17	TEL	Telephone call	$ 0.75	
4/17	FOOD	Restaurant	$35.25	
4/18	RMCH	Room charge	$88.00	
4/18	TAX1	Occupancy tax		
4/18	TAX2	Sales tax		
4/18	FOOD	Restaurant	$24.50	
4/19	RMCH	Room charge	$88.00	
4/19	TAX1	Occupancy tax		
4/19	TAX2	Sales tax		

SUMMARY

Description	No. of entries	Cost/entry	Total
Room charge			
Occupancy tax			
Sales tax			
Restaurant		—	
Telephone			
TOTALS	—	—	

Basic Computation Series 2000: Working with Percents
SECTION 3 Applications Involving Percents

Answers to Exercises

PAGE 5

1. $\frac{24}{100}, \frac{6}{25}$, 0.24 2. $\frac{56}{100}, \frac{14}{25}$, 0.56 3. $\frac{92}{100}, \frac{23}{25}$, 0.92 4. $\frac{105}{100}, \frac{21}{20}$, 1.05

5. $\frac{69}{100}, \frac{69}{100}$, 0.69 6. $\frac{53}{100}, \frac{53}{100}$, 0.53 7. $\frac{28}{100}, \frac{7}{25}$, 0.28 8. $\frac{75}{100}, \frac{3}{4}$, 0.75

9. $\frac{25}{100}, \frac{1}{4}$, 0.25 10. $\frac{50}{100}, \frac{1}{2}$, 0.50 11. $\frac{33\frac{1}{3}}{100}, \frac{1}{3}$, $0.\overline{3}$ 12. $\frac{32}{100}, \frac{8}{25}$, 0.32

13. $\frac{145}{100}, \frac{29}{20}$, 1.45 14. $\frac{62\frac{1}{2}}{100}, \frac{5}{8}$, 0.625 15. $\frac{176}{100}, \frac{44}{25}$, 1.76 16. $\frac{225}{100}, \frac{9}{4}$,

2.25 17. $\frac{95}{100}, \frac{19}{20}$, 0.95 18. $\frac{42}{100}, \frac{21}{50}$, 0.42 19. $\frac{265}{100}, \frac{53}{20}$, 2.65

20. $\frac{67}{100}, \frac{67}{100}$, 0.67

PAGE 6

1. $\frac{1}{2}$, 0.50, 50% 2. $\frac{1}{4}$, 0.25, 25% 3. $\frac{7}{4}$, 1.75, 175% 4. $\frac{7}{5}$, 1.40, 140% 5. $\frac{12}{5}$, 2.40, 240% 6. $\frac{17}{10}$, 1.70, 170% 7. $\frac{11}{20}$, 0.55, 55% 8. $\frac{27}{20}$, 1.35, 135% 9. $\frac{37}{20}$, 1.85, 185% 10. $\frac{51}{25}$, 2.04, 204% 11. $\frac{5}{4}$, 1.25, 125% 12. $\frac{3}{25}$, 0.12, 12% 13. $\frac{14}{25}$, 0.56, 56% 14. $\frac{22}{25}$, 0.88, 88% 15. $\frac{24}{25}$, 0.96, 96% 16. $\frac{36}{25}$, 1.44, 144% 17. $\frac{44}{25}$, 1.76, 176% 18. $\frac{53}{25}$, 2.12, 212% 19. $\frac{1}{5}$, 0.20, 20% 20. $\frac{9}{20}$, 0.45, 45%

PAGE 7

1. $\frac{68}{100}, \frac{17}{25}$, 0.68 2. $\frac{73}{100}, \frac{73}{100}$, 0.73 3. $\frac{46}{100}, \frac{23}{50}$, 0.46 4. $\frac{29}{100}, \frac{29}{100}$, 0.29 5. $\frac{50}{100}, \frac{1}{2}$, 0.50 6. $\frac{34}{100}, \frac{17}{50}$, 0.34 7. $\frac{26}{100}, \frac{13}{50}$, 0.26 8. $\frac{81}{100}, \frac{81}{100}$, 0.81 9. $\frac{49}{100}, \frac{49}{100}$, 0.49 10. $\frac{56}{100}, \frac{14}{25}$, 0.56 11. $\frac{59}{100}, \frac{59}{100}$, 0.59 12. $\frac{98}{100}, \frac{49}{50}$, 0.98 13. $\frac{156}{100}, \frac{39}{25}$, 1.56 14. $\frac{216}{100}, \frac{54}{25}$, 2.16 15. $\frac{44}{100}, \frac{11}{25}$, 0.44 16. $\frac{114}{100}, \frac{57}{50}$, 1.14 17. $\frac{29}{100}, \frac{29}{100}$, 0.29 18. $\frac{32}{100}, \frac{8}{25}$, 0.32

19. $\frac{67}{100}, \frac{67}{100}$, 0.67 20. $\frac{37\frac{1}{2}}{100}, \frac{3}{8}$, 0.375

PAGE 8

1. $\frac{49}{20}$, 2.45, 245% 2. $\frac{17}{20}$, 0.85, 85% 3. $\frac{9}{5}$, 1.80, 180% 4. $\frac{4}{25}$, 0.16, 16% 5. $\frac{6}{5}$, 1.20, 120% 6. $\frac{27}{10}$, 2.70, 270% 7. $\frac{76}{25}$, 3.04, 304% 8. $\frac{31}{20}$, 1.55, 155% 9. $\frac{7}{20}$, 0.35, 35% 10. $\frac{7}{10}$, 0.70, 70%

11. $\frac{9}{4}$, 2.25, 225% 12. $\frac{3}{2}$, 1.50, 150% 13. $\frac{33}{25}$, 1.32, 132% 14. $\frac{44}{25}$, 1.76, 176% 15. $\frac{8}{25}$, 0.32, 32% 16. $\frac{13}{25}$, 0.52, 52% 17. $\frac{32}{25}$, 1.28, 128% 18. $\frac{1}{5}$, 0.20, 20% 19. $\frac{3}{10}$, 0.30, 30% 20. $\frac{23}{10}$, 2.30, 230%

PAGE 9

1. $\frac{35}{100}, \frac{7}{20}$, 0.35 2. $\frac{60}{100}, \frac{3}{5}$, 0.60 3. $\frac{42}{100}, \frac{21}{50}$, 0.42 4. $\frac{28}{100}, \frac{7}{25}$, 0.28

5. $\frac{39}{100}, \frac{39}{100}$, 0.39 6. $\frac{37\frac{1}{2}}{100}, \frac{3}{8}$, 0.375 7. $\frac{40}{100}, \frac{2}{5}$, 0.40 8. $\frac{76}{100}, \frac{19}{25}$, 0.76

9. $\frac{53}{100}, \frac{53}{100}$, 0.53 10. $\frac{75}{100}, \frac{3}{4}$, 0.75 11. $\frac{65}{100}, \frac{13}{20}$, 0.65 12. $\frac{33\frac{1}{3}}{100}, \frac{1}{3}$,

$0.\overline{3}$ 13. $\frac{72}{100}, \frac{18}{25}$, 0.72 14. $\frac{150}{100}, \frac{3}{2}$, 1.50 15. $\frac{47}{100}, \frac{47}{100}$, 0.47

16. $\frac{12}{100}, \frac{3}{25}$, 0.12 17. $\frac{175}{100}, \frac{7}{4}$, 1.75 18. $\frac{67}{100}, \frac{67}{100}$, 0.67 19. $\frac{12\frac{1}{2}}{100}, \frac{1}{8}$,

0.125 20. $\frac{85}{100}, \frac{17}{20}$, 0.85

PAGE 10

1. $\frac{4}{5}$, 0.80, 80% 2. $\frac{19}{20}$, 0.95, 95% 3. $\frac{51}{20}$, 2.55, 255%

4. $\frac{11}{10}$, 1.10, 110% 5. $\frac{21}{20}$, 1.05, 105% 6. $\frac{43}{20}$, 2.15, 215%

7. $\frac{42}{25}$, 1.68, 168% 8. $\frac{28}{25}$, 1.12, 112% 9. $\frac{11}{25}$, 0.44, 44%

10. $\frac{34}{25}$, 1.36, 136% 11. $\frac{11}{4}$, 2.75, 275% 12. $\frac{1}{4}$, 0.25, 25%

13. $\frac{1}{20}$, 0.05, 5% 14. $\frac{21}{25}$, 0.84, 84% 15. $\frac{47}{25}$, 1.88, 188%

16. $\frac{9}{4}$, 2.25, 225% 17. $\frac{5}{2}$, 2.50, 250% 18. $\frac{8}{5}$, 1.60, 160%

19. $\frac{13}{20}$, 0.65, 65% 20. $\frac{11}{5}$, 2.20, 220%

PAGE 11

1. $\frac{102}{100}, \frac{51}{50}$, 1.02 2. $\frac{53}{100}, \frac{53}{100}$, 0.53 3. $\frac{30}{100}, \frac{3}{10}$, 0.30 4. $\frac{36}{100}, \frac{9}{25}$, 0.36

5. $\frac{69}{100}, \frac{69}{100}$, 0.69 6. $\frac{20}{100}, \frac{1}{5}$, 0.20 7. $\frac{5}{100}, \frac{1}{20}$, 0.05 8. $\frac{38}{100}, \frac{19}{50}$, 0.38

9. $\frac{25}{100}, \frac{1}{4}$, 0.25 10. $\frac{84}{100}, \frac{21}{25}$, 0.84 11. $\frac{62}{100}, \frac{31}{50}$, 0.62 12. $\frac{115}{100}, \frac{23}{20}$,

1.15 13. $\frac{48}{100}, \frac{12}{25}$, 0.48 14. $\frac{34}{100}, \frac{17}{50}$, 0.34 15. $\frac{81}{100}, \frac{81}{100}$, 0.81

16. $\frac{66\frac{2}{3}}{100}, \frac{2}{3}$, $0.\overline{6}$ 17. $\frac{325}{100}, \frac{13}{4}$, 3.25 18. $\frac{37\frac{1}{2}}{100}, \frac{3}{8}$, 0.375 19. $\frac{155}{100}, \frac{31}{20}$,

1.55 20. $\frac{12\frac{1}{2}}{100}, \frac{1}{8}$, 0.125

PAGE 12

1. $\frac{1}{5}$, 0.20, 20% 2. $\frac{7}{5}$, 1.40, 140% 3. $\frac{3}{2}$, 1.50, 150% 4. $\frac{21}{10}$, 2.10, 210% 5. $\frac{29}{20}$, 1.45, 145% 6. $\frac{23}{20}$, 1.15, 115% 7. $\frac{19}{25}$, 0.76, 76%

8. $\frac{44}{25}$, 1.76, 176% 9. $\frac{2}{25}$, 0.08, 8% 10. $\frac{3}{4}$, 0.75, 75% 11. $\frac{7}{4}$, 1.75, 175% 12. $\frac{9}{10}$, 0.90, 90% 13. $\frac{9}{5}$, 1.80, 180% 14. $\frac{41}{20}$, 2.05, 205%

15. $\frac{37}{25}$, 1.48, 148% 16. $\frac{49}{25}$, 1.96, 196% 17. $\frac{11}{50}$, 0.22, 22%

18. $\frac{6}{25}$, 0.24, 24% 19. $\frac{12}{5}$, 2.40, 240% 20. $\frac{33}{20}$, 1.65, 165%

PAGE 13

1. $\frac{28}{100}, \frac{7}{25}$, 0.28 2. $\frac{41}{100}, \frac{41}{100}$, 0.41 3. $\frac{53}{100}, \frac{53}{100}$, 0.53 4. $\frac{100}{100}, \frac{1}{1}$,

1.00 or 1 5. $\frac{48}{100}, \frac{12}{25}$, 0.48 6. $\frac{32}{100}, \frac{8}{25}$, 0.32 7. $\frac{81}{100}, \frac{81}{100}$, 0.81

8. $\frac{40}{100}, \frac{2}{5}$, 0.4 9. $\frac{7}{100}, \frac{7}{100}$, 0.07 10. $\frac{95}{100}, \frac{19}{20}$, 0.95 11. $\frac{82}{100}, \frac{41}{50}$,

0.82 12. $\frac{75}{100}, \frac{3}{4}$, 0.75 13. $\frac{42}{100}, \frac{21}{50}$, 0.42 14. $\frac{250}{100}, \frac{5}{2}$, 2.5 15. $\frac{125}{100}$,

$\frac{5}{4}$, 1.25 16. $\frac{33\frac{1}{3}}{100}, \frac{1}{3}$, $0.\overline{3}$ 17. $\frac{145}{100}, \frac{29}{20}$, 1.45 18. $\frac{12\frac{1}{2}}{100}, \frac{1}{8}$, 0.125

19. $\frac{112}{100}, \frac{28}{25}$, 1.12 20. $\frac{43}{100}, \frac{43}{100}$, 0.43

PAGE 14

1. $\frac{1}{4}$, 0.25, 25% 2. $\frac{2}{5}$, 0.4, 40% 3. $\frac{1}{10}$, 0.1, 10% 4. $\frac{13}{10}$, 1.3, 130% 5. $\frac{17}{20}$, 0.85, 85% 6. $\frac{5}{4}$, 1.25, 125% 7. $\frac{4}{5}$, 0.8, 80%

8. $\frac{9}{5}$, 1.8, 180% 9. $\frac{37}{20}$, 1.85, 185% 10. $\frac{1}{25}$, 0.04, 4%

11. $\frac{9}{25}$, 0.36, 36% 12. $\frac{26}{25}$, 1.04, 104% 13. $\frac{12}{25}$, 0.48, 48%

14. $\frac{23}{10}$, 2.3, 230% 15. $\frac{31}{25}$, 1.24, 124% 16. $\frac{16}{25}$, 0.64, 64%

17. $\frac{3}{20}$, 0.15, 15% 18. $\frac{11}{4}$, 2.75, 275% 19. $\frac{23}{20}$, 1.15, 115%

20. $\frac{49}{20}$, 2.45, 245%

PAGE 15

1. 21 **2.** 42 **3.** 75 **4.** 14 **5.** 57 **6.** 9 **7.** 12 **8.** 28 **9.** 54 **10.** 50
11. 51 **12.** 90 **13.** 33 **14.** 63 **15.** 39 **16.** 21 **17.** 42 **18.** 75
19. 14 **20.** 57 **21.** 9 **22.** 12 **23.** 28 **24.** 54 **25.** 50 **26.** 51
27. 90 **28.** 33 **29.** 63 **30.** 39

PAGE 16

1. 70 **2.** 168 **3.** 161 **4.** 252 **5.** 287 **6.** 70 **7.** 168 **8.** 161 **9.** 252
10. 287 **11.** 4.68 **12.** 14.28 **13.** 55 **14.** 8.96 **15.** 85.2 **16.** 30.24
17. 3.51 **18.** 24.84 **19.** 60.39 **20.** 65.65

PAGE 17

1. 12 **2.** 46 **3.** 72 **4.** 35 **5.** 34 **6.** 8 **7.** 16 **8.** 48 **9.** 68 **10.** 61
11. 12 **12.** 76 **13.** 20 **14.** 120 **15.** 160 **16.** 12 **17.** 46 **18.** 72
19. 35 **20.** 34 **21.** 8 **22.** 16 **23.** 48 **24.** 68 **25.** 61 **26.** 12
27. 76 **28.** 20 **29.** 120 **30.** 160

PAGE 18

1. 36 **2.** 99 **3.** 261 **4.** 180 **5.** 225 **6.** 36 **7.** 99 **8.** 261 **9.** 180
10. 225 **11.** 33.8 **12.** 180.34 **13.** 131.56 **14.** 45.39 **15.** 112.05
16. 22.08 **17.** 24.96 **18.** 93.96 **19.** 54.34 **20.** 110.4

PAGE 19

1. 21 **2.** 60 **3.** 168 **4.** 129 **5.** 273 **6.** 13 **7.** 48 **8.** 33 **9.** 94
10. 128 **11.** 27 **12.** 36 **13.** 39 **14.** 12 **15.** 69 **16.** 21 **17.** 60
18. 168 **19.** 129 **20.** 273 **21.** 13 **22.** 48 **23.** 33 **24.** 94 **25.** 128
26. 27 **27.** 36 **28.** 39 **29.** 12 **30.** 69

PAGE 20

1. 136 **2.** 68 **3.** 340 **4.** 323 **5.** 408 **6.** 136 **7.** 68 **8.** 340 **9.** 323
10. 408 **11.** 34.04 **12.** 15.81 **13.** 19.92 **14.** 112.75 **15.** 65.66
16. 60.84 **17.** 48.36 **18.** 31.46 **19.** 82.08 **20.** 16.77

PAGE 21

1. 10 **2.** 4 **3.** 18 **4.** 36 **5.** 29 **6.** 49 **7.** 21 **8.** 89 **9.** 107 **10.** 154
11. 70 **12.** 189 **13.** 245 **14.** 294 **15.** 371 **16.** 10 **17.** 4 **18.** 18
19. 36 **20.** 29 **21.** 49 **22.** 21 **23.** 89 **24.** 107 **25.** 154 **26.** 70
27. 189 **28.** 245 **29.** 294 **30.** 371

PAGE 22

1. 45 **2.** 72 **3.** 198 **4.** 135 **5.** 270 **6.** 45 **7.** 72 **8.** 198 **9.** 135
10. 270 **11.** 31.68 **12.** 30.21 **13.** 31.68 **14.** 48.26 **15.** 46.24
16. 55.08 **17.** 23.56 **18.** 24.94 **19.** 20.52 **20.** 44.08

PAGE 23

1. 28 **2.** 60 **3.** 48 **4.** 84 **5.** 180 **6.** 40 **7.** 50 **8.** 75 **9.** 45
10. 155 **11.** 90 **12.** 45 **13.** 126 **14.** 207 **15.** 315 **16.** 28 **17.** 60
18. 48 **19.** 84 **20.** 180 **21.** 40 **22.** 50 **23.** 75 **24.** 45 **25.** 155
26. 90 **27.** 45 **28.** 126 **29.** 207 **30.** 315

PAGE 24

1. 28 **2.** 126 **3.** 259 **4.** 203 **5.** 406 **6.** 28 **7.** 126 **8.** 259 **9.** 203
10. 406 **11.** 19.52 **12.** 41.34 **13.** 46.62 **14.** 15.54 **15.** 54.02
16. 29.7 **17.** 20.44 **18.** 40.48 **19.** 44.16 **20.** 51.52

PAGE 25

1. 50% **2.** $33\frac{1}{3}$% **3.** $66\frac{2}{3}$% **4.** 25% **5.** 75% **6.** 20% **7.** 40%
8. 60% **9.** 80% **10.** 140% **11.** $12\frac{1}{2}$% **12.** $37\frac{1}{2}$% **13.** $62\frac{1}{2}$%
14. $87\frac{1}{2}$% **15.** $112\frac{1}{2}$% **16.** 70% **17.** 30% **18.** 90% **19.** 125%
20. $137\frac{1}{2}$% **21.** 10 **22.** 30 **23.** 49 **24.** 36 **25.** 60 **26.** 5 **27.** 9
28. 8 **29.** 90 **30.** 22 **31.** 24 **32.** 20 **33.** 108 **34.** 154 **35.** 49
36. 535

PAGE 26

1. 0.48 **2.** 0.92 **3.** 0.56 **4.** 0.12 **5.** 0.59 **6.** 0.17 **7.** 0.87 **8.** 0.42
9. 0.31 **10.** 1.25 **11.** 1.67 **12.** 1.05 **13.** 1.10 **14.** 0.007 **15.** 0.03
16. 2.50 **17.** 7.00 **18.** 0.01 **19.** 0.175 **20.** 0.093 **21.** 13.92
22. 69.92 **23.** 11.16 **24.** 51.33 **25.** 48.3 **26.** 5.95 **27.** 37.41
28. 23.25 **29.** 115 **30.** 32.5 **31.** 70.14 **32.** 28.35 **33.** 2.268
34. 5.12 **35.** 3.85 **36.** 8.82

PAGE 27

1. $62\frac{1}{2}$% **2.** $33\frac{1}{3}$% **3.** 25% **4.** 137.5% **5.** 80% **6.** $66\frac{2}{3}$%
7. 125% **8.** 37.5% **9.** 375% **10.** 340% **11.** 75% **12.** 87.5%
13. 162.5% **14.** 70% **15.** $22\frac{2}{9}$% **16.** 180% **17.** 90% **18.** 60%
19. $166\frac{2}{3}$% **20.** 30% **21.** 38 **22.** 85 **23.** 81 **24.** 255 **25.** 147
26. 49 **27.** 212 **28.** 18 **29.** 50 **30.** 56 **31.** 224 **32.** 99 **33.** 105
34. 177 **35.** 72 **36.** 161

PAGE 28

1. 0.36 **2.** 0.57 **3.** 0.46 **4.** 0.08 **5.** 0.13 **6.** 0.31 **7.** 0.19 **8.** 0.16
9. 0.23 **10.** 1.32 **11.** 0.27 **12.** 0.054 **13.** 0.037 **14.** 0.081
15. 0.163 **16.** 0.082 **17.** 0.174 **18.** 0.136 **19.** 0.159 **20.** 0.281
21. 15.48 **22.** 15.96 **23.** 14.72 **24.** 18.59 **25.** 13.76 **26.** 8.99
27. 14.25 **28.** 64.68 **29.** 2.106 **30.** 1.776 **31.** 2.214 **32.** 3.402
33. 9.112 **34.** 8.586 **35.** 25.852 **36.** 1.98

PAGE 29

1. $37\frac{1}{2}$% **2.** 125% **3.** 160% **4.** $33\frac{1}{3}$% **5.** 325% **6.** 60%
7. 87.5% **8.** 25% **9.** $66\frac{2}{3}$% **10.** 70% **11.** 137.5% **12.** 50%
13. 40% **14.** 62.5% **15.** 80% **16.** 20% **17.** 30% **18.** $166\frac{2}{3}$%
19. 75% **20.** $55\frac{5}{9}$% **21.** 91 **22.** 55 **23.** 81 **24.** 38 **25.** 60
26. 112 **27.** 8 **28.** 33 **29.** 98 **30.** 108 **31.** 31 **32.** 80 **33.** 168
34. 75 **35.** 135 **36.** 41

PAGE 30

1. 0.26 **2.** 0.05 **3.** 0.16 **4.** 0.82 **5.** 0.08 **6.** 0.12 **7.** 0.29 **8.** 0.32
9. 0.09 **10.** 0.17 **11.** 0.069 **12.** 0.0762 **13.** 0.0031 **14.** 8.10
15. 0.096 **16.** 0.032 **17.** 0.0514 **18.** 0.0023 **19.** 0.003 **20.** 1.14
21. 22.62 **22.** 15.36 **23.** 13.12 **24.** 40.24 **25.** 348.3 **26.** 8.04
27. 16.24 **28.** 26.24 **29.** 21.87 **30.** 18.02 **31.** 2.208 **32.** 3.7522
33. 0.1219 **34.** 8.193 **35.** 33.06 **36.** 0.2412

PAGE 31

1. 90% 2. 12.5% 3. 130% 4. 125% 5. $11\frac{1}{9}$% 6. 225%
7. 25% 8. 75% 9. 37.5% 10. 87.5% 11. 40% 12. 212.5%
13. 62.5% 14. 325% 15. 70% 16. 140% 17. 187.5% 18. 50%
19. 180% 20. $122\frac{2}{9}$% 21. 6 22. 36 23. 21 24. 28 25. 75
26. 22 27. 126 28. 117 29. 11 30. 47 31. 153 32. 207
33. 195 34. 7 35. 155 36. 535

PAGE 32

1. 0.22 2. 0.13 3. 0.72 4. 0.81 5. 0.24 6. 0.69 7. 0.52 8. 0.55
9. 0.32 10. 1.37 11. 0.172 12. 0.181 13. 0.053 14. 1.13
15. 0.151 16. 0.092 17. 0.0035 18. 0.014 19. 0.095 20. 0.081
21. 17.82 22. 8.45 23. 9.88 24. 51.03 25. 14.4 26. 12.24
27. 20.16 28. 5.504 29. 2.715 30. 0.294 31. 11.476 32. 5.244
33. 2.1 34. 0.392 35. 63.28 36. 11.591

PAGE 33

1. 40% 2. $66\frac{2}{3}$% 3. 125% 4. 140% 5. 70% 6. $166\frac{2}{3}$%
7. 37.5% 8. 150% 9. 60% 10. 75% 11. 80% 12. $33\frac{1}{3}$%
13. 50% 14. 12.5% 15. 20% 16. 30% 17. 175% 18. $233\frac{1}{3}$%
19. $11\frac{1}{9}$% 20. 130% 21. 45 22. 63 23. 135 24. 33 25. 65
26. 52 27. 50 28. 135 29. 119 30. 12 31. 81 32. 161 33. 36
34. 10 35. 22 36. 45

PAGE 34

1. 0.42 2. 0.35 3. 0.58 4. 0.07 5. 0.16 6. 0.83 7. 0.09 8. 0.72
9. 0.77 10. 0.89 11. 0.122 12. 0.087 13. 1.15 14. 0.0032
15. 0.069 16. 0.035 17. 0.129 18. 0.052 19. 0.141 20. 0.0003
21. 39.48 22. 9.45 23. 36.54 24. 167.09 25. 64.8 26. 33.84
27. 65.17 28. 9.272 29. 29.145 30. 31.05 31. 0.2976 32. 7.038
33. 2.135 34. 6.837 35. 8.037 36. 0.345

PAGE 35

1. 3.84 2. 19 3. 12.09 4. 17 5. 30.71 6. 11 7. 7.381 8. 57
9. 8.487 10. 124 11. 96 12. 1.1096 13. 45 14. 10.152 15. 43
16. 1.26 17. 342 18. 62.568 19. 110 20. 5.916

PAGE 36

	Sales Tax	Total			Sales Tax	Total
1.	$2.30	$31.00		11.	$8.41	$113.55
2.	$4.49	$60.59		12.	$5.38	$72.68
3.	$3.61	$48.72		13.	$4.42	$59.63
4.	$5.06	$68.25		14.	$6.09	$82.22
5.	$2.18	$29.40		15.	$8.89	$119.99
6.	$7.47	$100.87		16.	$2.27	$30.59
7.	$5.38	$72.58		17.	$4.58	$61.88
8.	$8.00	$108.00		18.	$7.37	$99.50
9.	$6.01	$81.17		19.	$1.08	$14.64
10.	$7.06	$95.26		20.	$2.07	$27.97

PAGE 37

1. 4.76 2. 50.16 3. 23 4. 13.871 5. 1.792 6. 28 7. 7.524
8. 38.64 9. 72 10. 81.9 11. 288 12. 12.159 13. 31.05 14. 281
15. 12.16 16. 22.62 17. 260 18. 55.61 19. 49.383 20. 11.658

PAGE 38

	Sales Tax	Total			Sales Tax	Total
1.	$2.20	$31.56		11.	$3.78	$54.18
2.	$6.56	$94.06		12.	$8.05	$115.34
3.	$17.64	$252.80		13.	$5.02	$71.97
4.	$5.66	$81.18		14.	$7.38	$105.80
5.	$7.01	$100.41		15.	$5.80	$83.11
6.	$4.15	$59.48		16.	$10.89	$156.09
7.	$5.80	$83.16		17.	$6.61	$94.71
8.	$6.93	$99.36		18.	$1.88	$26.88
9.	$3.27	$46.83		19.	$3.22	$46.17
10.	$2.05	$29.43		20.	$5.02	$71.91

PAGE 39

1. 111.93 2. 16,438 3. 187.11 4. 63 5. 93.48 6. 882 7. 39.06
8. 348 9. 2.432 10. 1,689 11. 5.561 12. 99 13. 14.56 14. 8
15. 91.28 16. 333 17. 39.48 18. 854 19. 333 20. 17.48

PAGE 40

	Sales Tax	Total			Sales Tax	Total
1.	$2.54	$32.44		11.	$2.48	$31.63
2.	$14.22	$181.52		12.	$5.71	$72.85
3.	$4.45	$56.82		13.	$9.05	$115.54
4.	$8.35	$106.56		14.	$6.59	$84.10
5.	$22.30	$284.65		15.	$5.72	$73.02
6.	$6.20	$79.15		16.	$4.69	$59.91
7.	$7.26	$92.66		17.	$9.21	$117.53
8.	$3.19	$40.74		18.	$2.51	$32.07
9.	$0.86	$10.96		19.	$6.49	$82.82
10.	$3.60	$45.97		20.	$25.50	$325.50

PAGE 41

1. 10.956 2. 83 3. 246 4. 775 5. 96.74 6. 157.08 7. 40.32
8. 2,253 9. 408.28 10. 201 11. 46 12. 996 13. 4.992 14. 225
15. 12 16. 2.563 17. 500 18. 38.28 19. 334 20. 18

PAGE 42

	Sales Tax	Total			Sales Tax	Total
1.	$2.66	$50.98		**11.**	$4.81	$92.21
2.	$1.50	$28.80		**12.**	$3.49	$67.00
3.	$3.79	$72.74		**13.**	$4.25	$81.45
4.	$5.47	$104.97		**14.**	$8.49	$162.81
5.	$10.03	$192.40		**15.**	$4.96	$95.21
6.	$3.98	$76.29		**16.**	$2.61	$50.08
7.	$4.97	$95.33		**17.**	$5.07	$97.26
8.	$13.88	$266.21		**18.**	$4.14	$79.42
9.	$4.23	$81.14		**19.**	$3.67	$70.48
10.	$4.87	$93.37		**20.**	$1.77	$33.88

PAGE 43

1. 35.91 **2.** 993 **3.** 6.642 **4.** 4,632 **5.** 88.56 **6.** 421 **7.** 2.881 **8.** 1.728 **9.** 543 **10.** 202.34 **11.** 532 **12.** 24.7 **13.** 33 **14.** 16 **15.** 205.74 **16.** 222 **17.** 47.74 **18.** 500 **19.** 20.193 **20.** 581

PAGE 44

	Sales Tax	Total			Sales Tax	Total
1.	$0.37	$5.72		**11.**	$6.02	$92.02
2.	$1.23	$18.73		**12.**	$2.63	$40.13
3.	$3.87	$59.12		**13.**	$2.05	$31.35
4.	$2.55	$39.04		**14.**	$3.87	$59.12
5.	$5.75	$87.96		**15.**	$7.28	$111.28
6.	$7.36	$122.52		**16.**	$6.50	$99.42
7.	$1.95	$29.87		**17.**	$4.87	$74.37
8.	$7.43	$113.57		**18.**	$5.43	$82.98
9.	$2.48	$37.90		**19.**	$2.68	$40.90
10.	$6.17	$94.34		**20.**	$5.05	$77.16

PAGE 47

1. 50% **2.** 60% **3.** 25% **4.** 10% **5.** 80% **6.** 75% **7.** 30% **8.** 62.5% **9.** 40% **10.** 87.5% **11.** 80% **12.** 70% **13.** 50% **14.** 75% **15.** 62.5% **16.** 40% **17.** 30% **18.** 25% **19.** 60% **20.** 50%

PAGE 48

1. 27 **2.** 44 **3.** 56 **4.** 72 **5.** 81 **6.** 56 **7.** 14 **8.** 7 **9.** 81 **10.** 17 **11.** 75 **12.** 57

PAGE 49

1. $33\frac{1}{3}$% **2.** 75% **3.** 37.5% **4.** 60% **5.** 50% **6.** 80% **7.** $66\frac{2}{3}$% **8.** 62.5% **9.** 25% **10.** 70% **11.** 60% **12.** 62.5% **13.** 90% **14.** 50% **15.** 25% **16.** 70% **17.** 75% **18.** 37.5% **19.** 30% **20.** 40%

PAGE 50

1. 56 **2.** 29 **3.** 16 **4.** 93 **5.** 51 **6.** 31 **7.** 57 **8.** 57 **9.** 85 **10.** 27 **11.** 96 **12.** 51

PAGE 51

1. 90% **2.** 62.5% **3.** $66\frac{2}{3}$% **4.** 60% **5.** 50% **6.** $33\frac{1}{3}$% **7.** 37.5% **8.** 75% **9.** 15% **10.** $58\frac{1}{3}$% **11.** 80% **12.** 40% **13.** 90% **14.** 110% **15.** 50% **16.** 150% **17.** 60% **18.** 200% **19.** 30% **20.** 20%

PAGE 52

1. 34 **2.** 16 **3.** 15 **4.** 27 **5.** 92 **6.** 48 **7.** 8 **8.** 16 **9.** 29 **10.** 5 **11.** 72 **12.** 21

PAGE 53

1. 60% **2.** 30% **3.** 75% **4.** $33\frac{1}{3}$% **5.** 87.5% **6.** 62.5% **7.** $28\frac{4}{7}$% **8.** 70% **9.** $66\frac{2}{3}$% **10.** 90% **11.** 50% **12.** 300% **13.** 150% **14.** 120% **15.** 75% **16.** 80% **17.** $33\frac{1}{3}$% **18.** $33\frac{1}{3}$% **19.** 70% **20.** 62.5%

PAGE 54

1. 27 **2.** 13 **3.** 41 **4.** 56 **5.** 23 **6.** 97 **7.** 52 **8.** 72 **9.** 48 **10.** 13 **11.** 56 **12.** 51

PAGE 55

1. 60% **2.** $33\frac{1}{3}$% **3.** 50% **4.** 62.5% **5.** 80% **6.** 25% **7.** $66\frac{2}{3}$% **8.** 37.5% **9.** 70% **10.** 35% **11.** 50% **12.** $33\frac{1}{3}$% **13.** 25% **14.** 25% **15.** 50% **16.** 75% **17.** 30% **18.** 150% **19.** $66\frac{2}{3}$% **20.** 50%

PAGE 56

1. 45 **2.** 17 **3.** 30 **4.** 75 **5.** 58 **6.** 85 **7.** 16 **8.** 54 **9.** 27 **10.** 94 **11.** 42 **12.** 17

PAGE 57

1. 14% **2.** 12 **3.** 30.34 **4.** 16 **5.** $33\frac{1}{3}$% **6.** 49 **7.** 11 **8.** 29% **9.** 53% **10.** 120 **11.** 8.46

PAGE 58

1. 25% **2.** 13.12 **3.** 47% **4.** 64 **5.** 54.81 **6.** 29% **7.** 75 **8.** 33 **9.** 59 **10.** 46 **11.** 30

Basic Computation Series 2000: Working with Percents
ANSWERS TO EXERCISES

94

PAGE 59

1. 89 **2.** 21 **3.** 6.3 **4.** 90 **5.** 62% **6.** 18 **7.** 20 **8.** $62\frac{1}{2}$% **9.** 85
10. 34.8 **11.** $66\frac{2}{3}$%

PAGE 60

1. 48.6 **2.** 32 **3.** 48% **4.** 46 **5.** 46 **6.** 46.44 **7.** 40 **8.** $33\frac{1}{3}$%
9. 27.36 **10.** 36 **11.** 29%

PAGE 61

1. 43% **2.** 44 **3.** 20.52 **4.** 75% **5.** 59 **6.** 45% **7.** 24 **8.** 3
9. 19.78 **10.** $37\frac{1}{2}$% **11.** 52

PAGE 62

1. 16% **2.** 124 **3.** 75 **4.** 76 **5.** $33\frac{1}{3}$% **6.** 14.82 **7.** 48% **8.** 90
9. 30 **10.** 52% **11.** 124

PAGE 63

1. 75% **2.** 42 **3.** 8 **4.** 32% **5.** 50 **6.** 60% **7.** 48 **8.** 12 **9.** 29.4
10. 37% **11.** 112

PAGE 64

1. 4.8 **2.** 85 **3.** 75% **4.** 56 **5.** 12.32 **6.** 25% **7.** 7.31 **8.** 108
9. 83% **10.** 52 **11.** 75%

PAGE 65

1. 98 **2.** 10% **3.** 95.12 **4.** 124 **5.** 32% **6.** 29 **7.** 43.2
8. $62\frac{1}{2}$% **9.** 6.45 **10.** 57% **11.** 132

PAGE 66

1. 57% **2.** 8.82 **3.** 92 **4.** 35 **5.** 43% **6.** 104 **7.** 9.72 **8.** 60%
9. 72 **10.** 61% **11.** 5.6

PAGE 71

1. Savings: $8.67; Sale Price: $49.11 **2.** Savings: $3.89; Sale Price:
$35.01 **3.** Savings: $14.18; Sale Price: $21.27 **4.** Savings: $5.49;
Sale Price: $16.47 **5.** Savings: $5.40; Sale Price: $24.58 **6.** Savings:
$11.40; Sale Price: $17.10 **7.** Savings: $5.93; Sale Price: $13.82
8. Savings: $11.00; Sale Price: $16.50

PAGE 72

1. Savings: $7.50; Sale Price: $30.00 **2.** Savings: $10.00; Sale Price:
$20.00 **3.** Savings: $25.00; Sale Price: $37.50 **4.** Savings: $3.25;
Sale Price: $29.25 **5.** Savings: $8.40; Sale Price: $33.60 **6.** Savings:
$8.00; Sale Price: $56.00 **7.** Savings: $4.05; Sale Price: $22.95
8. Savings: $1.85; Sale Price: $16.65

PAGE 73

1. Savings: $26.39; Sale Price: $193.56 **2.** Savings: $11.35; Sale
Price: $34.05 **3.** Savings: $6.45; Sale Price: $15.05 **4.** Savings:
$5.70; Sale Price: $22.80 **5.** Savings: $43.67; Sale Price: $154.83
6. Savings: $4.30; Sale Price: $17.20 **7.** Savings: $3.90; Sale Price:
$22.10 **8.** Savings: $8.10; Sale Price: $18.90

PAGE 74

1. Savings: $31.10; Sale Price: $62.20 **2.** Savings: $8.10; Sale Price:
$24.30 **3.** Savings: $6.10; Sale Price: $42.70 **4.** Savings: $16.80;
Sale Price: $25.20 **5.** Savings: $9.70; Sale Price: $38.80 **6.** Savings:
$8.45; Sale Price: $76.05 **7.** Savings: $21.20; Sale Price: $42.40
8. Savings: $3.00; Sale Price: $21.00

PAGE 75

1. Savings: $10.13; Sale Price: $28.82 **2.** Savings: $23.98; Sale
Price: $35.97 **3.** Savings: $7.20; Sale Price: $21.60 **4.** Savings:
$7.77; Sale Price: $18.13 **5.** Savings: $33.50; Sale Price: $126.00
6. Savings: $2.82; Sale Price: $15.98 **7.** Savings: $1.98; Sale Price:
$17.82 **8.** Savings: $8.00; Sale Price: $24.00

PAGE 76

1. Savings: $6.58; Sale Price: $59.22 **2.** Savings: $11.70; Sale Price:
$27.30 **3.** Savings: $13.66; Sale Price: $27.32 **4.** Savings: $12.50;
Sale Price: $18.75 **5.** Savings: $11.84; Sale Price: $35.52 **6.** Savings:
$25.83; Sale Price: $51.66 **7.** Savings: $5.45; Sale Price: $21.80
8. Savings: $7.70; Sale Price: $15.40

PAGE 77

1. Savings: $11.12; Sale Price: $74.38 **2.** Savings: $7.99; Sale Price:
$31.96 **3.** Savings: $1.75; Sale Price: $15.75 **4.** Savings: $8.10;
Sale Price: $24.30 **5.** Savings: $37.50; Sale Price: $112.50
6. Savings: $5.86; Sale Price: $17.58 **7.** Savings: $5.10; Sale Price:
$20.40 **8.** Savings: $5.26; Sale Price: $21.04

PAGE 78

1. Savings: $28.90; Sale Price: $43.35 **2.** Savings: $9.75; Sale Price:
$39.00 **3.** Savings: $15.85; Sale Price: $47.55 **4.** Savings: $2.94;
Sale Price: $26.46 **5.** Savings: $5.94; Sale Price: $33.66 **6.** Savings:
$14.58; Sale Price: $34.02 **7.** Savings: $5.50; Sale Price: $22.00
8. Savings: $3.50; Sale Price: $14.00

PAGE 79

1. Savings: $32.55; Sale Price: $184.45 **2.** Savings: $9.99; Sale
Price: $39.96 **3.** Savings: $8.00; Sale Price: $24.00 **4.** Savings:
$2.85; Sale Price: $25.65 **5.** Savings: $8.10; Sale Price: $36.90
6. Savings: $2.15; Sale Price: $19.35 **7.** Savings: $6.86; Sale Price:
$20.58 **8.** Savings: $5.25; Sale Price: $29.75

PAGE 80

1. Savings: $9.90; Sale Price: $39.60 **2.** Savings: $10.55; Sale Price:
$31.65 **3.** Savings: $7.70; Sale Price: $30.80 **4.** Savings: $11.78;
Sale Price: $17.67 **5.** Savings: $5.64; Sale Price: $31.96 **6.** Savings:
$14.70; Sale Price: $58.80 **7.** Savings: $7.14; Sale Price: $21.42
8. Savings: $1.65; Sale Price: $14.85

PAGE 81

	item	amount saved	percent saved
1.	computer package	$398.00	30.66%
2.	flatbed scanner	$30.00	33.34%
3.	spreadsheet program	$20.00	33.34%
4.	file crate	$2.00	33.39%
5.	computer work station	$20.00	20%
6.	desk chair	$20.00	11.77%
7.	color jet printer	$30.00	25%

PAGE 82

GUEST'S STATEMENT

Description	Charge	Balance
Room charge	$79.00	$79.00
Occupancy tax	$7.90	$86.90
Sales tax	$6.32	$93.22
Telephone call	$0.75	$93.97
Restaurant	$35.75	$129.72
Room charge	$79.00	$208.72
Occupancy tax	$7.90	$216.62
Sales tax	$6.32	$222.94
Restaurant	$46.12	$269.06
Room charge	$79.00	$348.06
Occupancy tax	$7.90	$355.96
Sales tax	$6.32	$362.28

SUMMARY

Description	No.	Cost/entry	Total
Room charge	3	$79.00	$237.00
Occupancy tax	3	$7.90	$23.70
Sales tax	3	$6.32	$18.96
Restaurant	2	—	$81.87
Telephone	1	$0.75	$0.75
TOTALS	—	—	$362.28

PAGE 83

	item	amount saved	percent saved
1.	35-mm camera	$30.00	27.28%
2.	35-mm film	$2.00	33.39%
3.	flashlight	$2.50	15.63%
4.	flashlight batteries	$1.60	34.86%
5.	classic videos	$2.00	11.12%
6.	designer watches	$3.00	10.35%
7.	CD boombox	$20.00	25%

PAGE 84

GUEST'S STATEMENT

Description	Charge	Balance
Room charge	$88.50	$88.50
Occupancy tax	$8.85	$97.35
Sales tax	$7.08	$104.43
Telephone call	$0.75	$105.18
Restaurant	$27.95	$133.13
Room charge	$88.50	$221.63
Occupancy tax	$8.85	$230.48
Sales tax	$7.08	$237.56
Room charge	$88.50	$326.06
Occupancy tax	$8.85	$334.91
Sales tax	$7.08	$341.99
Restaurant	$57.16	$399.15

SUMMARY

Description	No.	Cost/entry	Total
Room charge	3	$88.50	$265.50
Occupancy tax	3	$8.85	$26.55
Sales tax	3	$7.08	$21.24
Restaurant	2	—	$85.11
Telephone	1	$0.75	$0.75
TOTALS	—	—	$399.15

item	amount saved	percent saved
1. shampoo	$1.19	32.25%
2. hair spray	$1.00	21.79%
3. toothpaste	$1.00	16.69%
4. bath soap	$0.10	11.24%
5. face soap	$0.30	23.26%
6. fragrance	$4.01	22.91%
7. paper towels	$0.30	18.87%

item	amount saved	percent saved
1. sweaters	$11.40	30%
2. shirts	$11.01	30.58%
3. leather coats	$130.01	50%
4. corduroy pants	$5.01	11.13%
5. jeans	$14.01	25.94%
6. running shoes	$22.01	25.89%
7. sweatshirts	$11.60	40%

GUEST'S STATEMENT

Description	Charge	Balance
Room charge	$104.00	$104.00
Occupancy tax	$10.40	$114.40
Sales tax	$8.32	$122.72
Telephone call	$0.75	$123.47
Restaurant	$28.95	$152.42
Room charge	$104.00	$256.42
Occupancy tax	$10.40	$266.82
Sales tax	$8.32	$275.14
Restaurant	$38.60	$313.74
Room charge	$104.00	$417.74
Occupancy tax	$10.40	$428.14
Sales tax	$8.32	$436.46

GUEST'S STATEMENT

Description	Charge	Balance
Room charge	$62.50	$62.50
Occupancy tax	$6.25	$68.75
Sales tax	$5.00	$73.75
Room charge	$62.50	$136.25
Occupancy tax	$6.25	$142.50
Sales tax	$5.00	$147.50
Restaurant	$42.45	$189.95
Room charge	$62.50	$252.45
Occupancy tax	$6.25	$258.70
Sales tax	$5.00	$263.70
Restaurant	$28.49	$292.19
Telephone call	$0.75	$292.94

SUMMARY

Description	No.	Cost/entry	Total
Room charge	3	$104.00	$312.00
Occupancy tax	3	$10.40	$31.20
Sales tax	3	$8.32	$24.96
Restaurant	2	—	$67.55
Telephone	1	$0.75	$0.75
TOTALS	—	—	$436.46

SUMMARY

Description	No.	Cost/entry	Total
Room charge	3	$62.50	$187.50
Occupancy tax	3	$6.25	$18.75
Sales tax	3	$5.00	$15.00
Restaurant	2	—	$70.94
Telephone	1	$0.75	$0.75
TOTALS	—	—	$292.94

PAGE 89

item	amount saved	percent saved
1. sweaters	$17.01	40.5%
2. jackets	$19.01	27.55%
3. shirts	$7.00	20%
4. slacks	$5.01	13.18%
5. jeans	$6.00	20%
6. boots	$10.96	21.94%
7. dress shoes	$7.45	16.21%

PAGE 90

GUEST'S STATEMENT

Description	Charge	Balance
Room charge	$88.00	$88.00
Occupancy tax	$8.80	$96.80
Sales tax	$7.04	$103.84
Telephone call	$0.75	$104.59
Restaurant	$35.25	$139.84
Room charge	$88.00	$227.84
Occupancy tax	$8.80	$236.64
Sales tax	$7.04	$243.68
Restaurant	$24.50	$268.18
Room charge	$88.00	$356.18
Occupancy tax	$8.80	$364.98
Sales tax	$7.04	$372.02

SUMMARY

Description	No.	Cost/entry	Total
Room charge	3	$88.00	$264.00
Occupancy tax	3	$8.80	$26.40
Sales tax	3	$7.04	$21.12
Restaurant	2	—	$59.75
Telephone	1	$0.75	$0.75
TOTALS	—	—	$372.02